MW00772426

RAISE
Your
Value

---

5 Steps for Architecture and Engineering Firms to Uncover Hidden Value, Design a Winning Advantage and Charge More

---

June R. Jewell, CPA

RAISE Your Value: 5 Steps for Architecture and Engineering Firms to Uncover Hidden Value, Design a Winning Advantage and Charge More

© Copyright 2022, JKL Publishing, LLC, Reston, Virginia, U.S.

For more information, email jjewell@aecbusiness.com

ISBN 978-0-9883824-4-2

How to Use This Book

This book was designed to give you a real, actionable process to uncover your hidden value and design a Winning Advantage so you can charge what you're really worth.

In just a few hours, you will have all the steps, tools, and hopefully motivation to take action and RAISE your firm's real and perceived value.

Access Free Resources Online:

✓ Take the Value Quotient (VQ) Assessment at https://www.aecbusiness.com/RAISEYourValue/VQ and see how your firm scores at valuing your work and getting paid what you're worth.

✓ Access all the free worksheets, tools, checklists and exercises.

✓ Sign up to receive invitations to free live and virtual special events and training opportunities for your team.

Access these and other resources at:

www.aecbusiness.com/RAISEYourValue/Resources

Get Your Resources

Table of Contents

Acknowledgements

This book would not be half of what it is without the help of so many brilliant friends, business experts, colleagues, and clients who offered their unique voices to such an important topic. I want to thank the following friends, colleagues, and industry authorities for their generous contributions to this book (in alphabetical order):

Amber Aguayo
Helen Apostolico
Ellen Bensky
Jeb Blount
Christi Bradbury
Robert Brewer
Michael T. Buell
Marjorie Burdetsky
Scott Butcher
J. Bruce Camino
Joel Carson
Jon Christensen
Chad Clinehans
Michael Davis
Kurt Fraese
Matt Garber
Michael V. Geary
Steve Gido
Steve Gordon
Charles H. Green
Jeff Henson
Jacob Hillmann
Andrea P. Howe
Mark Hunter
Ursula Iafrate
Lee James
Lisa Wallis-Dutra

Bryan Johnson
Ganesh Kadam
Bob Kelleher
Roman Kmenta
Ray Kogan
Rob Lamb
Gabe Lett
Frank Lippert
John Lowe
Geralanne Maglione
Nick Mannel
Perry Marshall
Kathryn Ness
Jen Newman
Paul Nowicki
David Phillips
Douglas Reed
Richard Rehmann
Jim Rogers
Russ Sanford
Kathleen M. Sharman
Kevin Sombart
David Stone
Ryan Suydam
Mike Trotta
Maria Vedral
Skip Weisman

Foreword

During the past 35 years in the architecture and engineering (A&E) industry I have watched with deep frustration the slow deterioration in the assumed level of prestige and value of our services. While clients push us to compete on price, we fear losing, especially during recessions, so we race to the bottom of the pricing curve without considering our value proposition. Then, we work extraordinary hours – many times without charging projects – in an effort to meet ridiculously low budgets. This approach can make our work unsatisfying and stressful, which in turn results in unengaged employees who are constantly looking for better employment options.

I believe that we bring enormous value to our clients, and even beyond that, we pay a great service to people's lives throughout the world. While A&E companies have a long history of striving for excellence in the work that is so critical to human survival, it is time for us to focus on ways we can deliver excellence in how we lead our companies. In turn, we can regain some of the confidence and stature that the industry has lost during the most recent decade and recognize the value our services provide.

June Jewell's new book, RAISE Your Value, provides a strong argument for increasing our perceived and delivered value, as well as a clear path to transforming your firm into a highly valued consulting practice with better clients and higher fees.

Our company, Kleinschmidt Associates, provides a strong case study of how the application of these concepts can dramatically impact your sales success and financial results. In 2017 we reached out to June for business training as part of our Kleinschmidt University Leadership Academy.

Following several years of decreasing win rates in our competitive pursuits, we recognized that we were investing significant time pursuing projects with clients where we had no solid relationships. Our Go/No-Go (GNG) process was not effective, and much of our energy was put into price- based bidding for thankless clients.

As a result of our work with June, we identified the culture traps holding us to the same ways of thinking. In turn, this recognition enabled us to transform our sales process to focus on our best clients, including:

- Categorizing our top 40+ clients (by revenue) into A, B, C, etc., and instantly implementing a No-Go on pursuits with any clients below level C.

- Ending relationships with two high revenue clients who were price-based, and otherwise difficult to work with – our toughest step, but an important statement to ourselves that we could do this and still succeed.

- Creating a Foundational Client list made up of mainly Type A and B clients and developing proactive relationship-development plans to ensure we had strong and deep relationships.

- Added the 'Existing or Anticipated Client Rank' to our GNG worksheet to minimize the chance of falling into our old culture traps.

Our Foundational Client focus (Client Categories), along with other improvements in our Business Development and Sales Process (improved Client Management Training, marketing collateral, social media use and GNG Processes) dramatically altered our sales success. As you can see from the metrics below, we significantly reduced our active pursuits while improving our New Work Won by 5-fold:

- 2016 – 137 pursuits, $2.3M Won

- 2017 – 155 pursuits, $4.4M Won

- 2018 – 113 pursuits, $9.8M Won

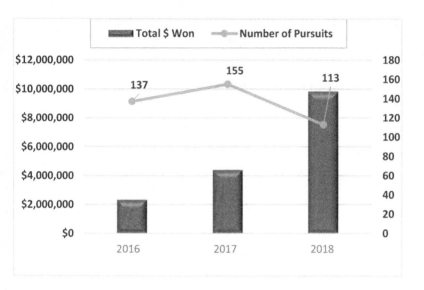

What we learned from our experience working with June and implementing the concepts she summarizes in this book is that these activities create a synergistic circle of opportunity. By focusing on our foundational clients, we treat them better. By limiting our pursuits for difficult clients or price-based opportunities, we have more time available to pursue really exciting projects. By winning exciting projects, our employees became more engaged. Together, all these factors lead to better results. Over the past 5 years, by following this approach, we've seen our New Work Won increase to over $40M and we've almost doubled in size from 120 employees in 2017 to over 220 in 2022.

These changes were intimidating at first – imagine severing ties with a client who represents 5-10% of your annual revenue. And at times, the process can seem overwhelming. However, I am confident that if you follow the steps outlined in this book, you can replicate this level of success. The 5-Step RAISE Your Value Formula is a simple, clearly defined approach to achieving exactly what Kleinschmidt achieved in less than a year, and it continues to build success today.

Get your entire team on board and make the RAISE Your Value approach part of your culture and values. You will not regret it!

Jon Christensen, President / CEO
Kleinschmidt Associates

Introduction

Be too expensive for crappy clients.

Why is it that some architecture and engineering (A&E) firms charge high fees and generate profits over 30% while others settle for 8-12% profits or less? Could it be that these successful firms have a "magic formula" to attract better, high paying clients? If your profits are not over 20%, if you've been competing on price, or if you struggle to get clients to pay what you are worth, this book is for you!

Highly educated and talented professionals should never be thrown into the same bucket with each other and forced to undersell their services. All professionals and firms are different, and it is up to you to decide what you are willing and not willing to do to get clients to hire you. No one ever started an A&E firm to become a commodity. Now is the time to raise your prices and become more selective about what you do and who you work with. Life is too short to work with jerks and cheapskates for low margins!

Since 1990 when I started my first company, Jewell & Associates, helping A&E firms implement Wind2 and Deltek business management software, the nation has experienced five economic peaks and valleys. Most A&E firms have ridden the roller coaster of multiple recessions and boom markets during which they alternated between layoffs and talent shortages, pay cuts and salary escalation, pricing pressure and, in the worst cases, bankruptcy.

Unfortunately, bad habits started to come out of the lean times - painful practices like taking unprofitable projects, working for ungrateful clients, and lowering fees to compete. Even when times were booming, A&E firms continued these practices, not recognizing a way to get and keep better clients. These behaviors are a form of self-sabotage.

Unbelievably, there are still an incredible number of A&E firms focused more on winning and delivering work than on actually making a profit. A&E professionals often avoid talking about money. Some don't value what they do for their clients, or their impact on the world. When they do understand the true impact of their services on communities, the environment and stakeholders, they use that as an excuse to take their focus off the financial results of projects, almost ashamed to make a profit on their passion projects.

This lack of focus on financial results has caused A&E services to become commoditized by clients—treating A&E firms as if they are easily replaceable and undervaluing their services, with price being the only meaningful differentiator between firms.

Some clients will force you to compete on price instead of qualifications or value. Clients put constant pressure on your staff to lower fees, do work out of the scope for free, and take on more project risk than is worth the profits you are earning. This leaves your staff frustrated and afraid to raise prices, even as salaries and other business costs are rapidly rising.

The real difference between the firms that lower their fees and those that charge top dollar is their focus on getting great clients, and their ability to understand and communicate their unique value. A bigger problem than your clients not valuing your work is your *team* not valuing your work! This book is designed to help you break this cycle by uncovering and leveraging your hidden value, because you have been keeping it a secret for too long.

You are giving your clients million-dollar ideas and advice every day – advice that saves them millions in construction costs, maintenance, avoiding problems, and risk. How can you put an hourly rate on that type of expertise?

Competing on price is limiting your growth and success. Low profits prohibit you from hiring top talent, offering competitive salaries and benefits, and investing in technology, acquisitions, marketing and business strategies to help you grow. Low profits also prevent you from stockpiling cash that will be needed for founder retirement, recessions or other unforeseen problems, like a pandemic. With continued low profits, your shareholders will not earn the return on investment they deserve for the risk they are taking or realize high multiples if you choose to sell. Low profits limit your firm's value.

This is the most prolific obstacle to your firm's success. Once you have allowed your clients to talk down your fees and refuse to pay what you are worth, it is hard to change.

But there is a straightforward way to elevate your firm out of this commoditization trap and become the valued, highly paid advisor you want and deserve to be. This book, and the 5-Step RAISE Your Value Formula you will learn, will be your guiding light to design your unique Winning Advantage in your marketplace.

For over 30 years I have been helping A&E firms fight commoditization. When I started working with A&E firms in Washington, DC in 1990, times were lean and competing on price was the norm. My focus was on helping firms reduce costs by increasing efficiency, automating financial management, and getting employees to follow business best practices (timesheets, change orders, etc.). My work in recent years has been focused on changing the mindset of A&E professionals to value their work and get paid based on the value they bring to clients.

In 1996, I was hired to help a 30-person engineering firm implement the Wind2 Financial Management System (FMS). Their goal was to automate their manual accounting and project management processes. When helping them set up their billing rate tables on hourly projects, I realized their rates were very low and did not cover their costs, much less generate a profit. They were losing money on every hour they worked. The rates had not been increased in years so this was a chronic problem.

When I reviewed this apparent "error" with them, they admitted that most of their clients were very tight on money, but they really enjoyed the projects, and couldn't increase the rates. They were effectively financing their clients' projects – with zero profit rates and waiting 140 days to get paid! While they were apprehensive to address this, I helped them develop a strategy to demonstrate to clients their value and show that no other firm could do what they had done. Their clients agreed to a 20% increase in rates, and they were finally making money on those projects after almost eight years.

After this experience, I started to see this issue in many of the clients I worked with. In fact, it was such a huge problem that it started to be discussed at industry conferences as the "commoditization of the A&E industry".

My mission with this book is to elevate the A&E industry and help firms achieve well-deserved rewards for the extraordinary impact they have on their clients, communities and the world.

In my first book, *Find the Lost Dollars: 6 Steps to Increase Profits in Architecture, Engineering and Environmental Firms*, I lay the groundwork for eliminating ineffective business practices caused by ten insidious culture traps. The Find the Lost Dollars book and corresponding training program are focused on improving employee performance, business processes, and use of systems to increase profits. But they did not go far enough to change the fundamental problem faced by most A&E firms – how to get paid what they are worth.

Several years ago, I created a workshop called *Selling on Value Instead of Price* where I helped firm leaders and their teams explore their true value and taught them how to communicate to get better clients and higher fees. **RAISE Your Value** came out of this work and provides a roadmap for diving into your firm's unique value so you can work for the best clients in your industry and charge top industry fees. *That* is your Winning Advantage.

After working with over a thousand A&E firms, I have seen the damage that failure to differentiate creates. I am passionate about turning around the mindset, business practices, and behaviors of A&E leaders and their staff to ensure they stop leaving money on the table. Implementation of this groundbreaking advice can catapult your firm into high-performing profit margins over 20%.

While the theories and methods provided in this book apply to every professional services business, I specifically focus on architecture and engineering firms that have struggled raising their prices. Whether you are architects or engineers, environmental consultants, management consultants, a marketing agency, CPA firm, government contractor, or sole service provider, you will get priceless strategies that will result in higher profits.

While high profits are important, the rewards you seek are not all monetary. There are many other benefits to learning to RAISE Your Value - better clients that appreciate you, happier employees that want to stay at your firm, and significantly higher win rates with less proposals.

These benefits can be achieved by knowing who your ideal client is, what they value, and charging top dollar for delivering superior results. Instead of lowering rates to win business, you can elevate your firm to the top of the selection process by talking differently and demonstrating your Unique Value Proposition.

Think about your best client. What is it that you love about them? Are they more fun to work with? Do they say thank you and appreciate your extra efforts? Do they accept your proposals and not try to get you to lower your fees? A great client is all this and more.

And what does a great client provide your firm? High profits – often above 20%, much happier employees that want to work hard and stay at your firm and repeat business that is easy to get.

What if every client could be like your best client? This book helps make that dream scenario possible. Imagine that the phone is ringing off the hook at your firm. Dozens of clients are calling every day begging to work with you, because you are the best. What would you do? Would you take every client and project that comes along? Or would this force you to be more selective?

RAISE Your Value: 5 Steps for Architecture and Engineering Firms to Uncover Hidden Value, Design a Winning Advantage and Charge More is a roadmap for achieving top industry profits and happier clients and employees. Together, we will uncover your unique value that gives you a Winning Advantage in project pursuits. We will change your firm's culture and paradigm from being a commodity, to being a valued advisor that clients will seek out and pay top dollar to work with. In this book, I present my groundbreaking 5-Step RAISE Your Value Formula. This practical and easy to follow program will help transform your culture, business practices and financial results.

Selling can be difficult for even the most experienced and trained seller. In most A&E firms, sales are conducted by seller-doers - technical professionals that often despise the idea of sales. We will help you reframe the idea of sales so your seller-doers will enjoy sales conversations and feel more confident and prepared having them.

This book will reveal 10 key principles to raise your firm's value in the minds of your clients and staff and design a Winning Advantage that will help you charge more for your services, get better clients that align with your values, and win more often. After you understand the 10 key principles, you will be in the perfect position to implement the 5-Step RAISE Your Value formula described in Chapter 10.

The 5-Step RAISE Your Value Formula as shown in the graphic below will transform your firm from where you are now, to a firm with a value-based culture where your employees are aligned around delivering and selling on value, not price.

Chapter 10 will outline what it will take for you to implement the 5-Step RAISE Your Value formula. While you can skip ahead to that chapter, it is much more effective if you read this book all the way through to fully immerse yourself in what it takes to design a Winning Advantage. The RAISE Your Value Formula is my Proprietary Process based on the acronym in the word RAISE. It simply involves **Rating** your clients and defining your ideal client criteria, **Assessing** your firm's current market position, project financials and selling practices, **Investigating** where you add unique value and designing a Winning Advantage, **Strategizing** how to get your new value proposition into the market and **Executing** on that strategic plan.

Your Winning Advantage is a combination of two new tools you will learn to create in this book, your Unique Value Proposition (UVP) and your exclusive Proprietary Process. You can think of your UVP as your elevator speech that is a compelling statement about your unique value that will appeal to your ideal clients. Your Proprietary Process is an acronym that you will learn how to develop that will differentiate and propel your firm to the top of selection lists. As they realize they can't get your UVP and Proprietary Process anywhere else, you will wildly attract ideal clients who pay top dollar for your elite expertise.

5-STEP RAISE YOUR VALUE FORMULA
Uncover Hidden Value, Design a Winning Advantage and Charge More

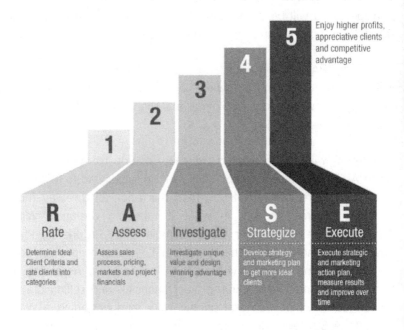

As I have learned in years of helping A&E firms improve and increase profits, execution is always the toughest part of change. To be successful, you will need to define and communicate your values and get your employees engaged in deep conversations about ideal clients, the results you deliver for them, and how to communicate your value effectively. You will need to change the way you talk with clients, write marketing messages and proposals, negotiate your contracts, and select which projects to take or walk away from. This may be difficult for professionals who have been doing things the same way their entire careers.

But the rewards justify the effort. And if you are diligent and apply the principles I discuss, it doesn't have to take long. My goal with this book is to help you get there in six months or less.

To aid your transformation, I have provided an abundance of worksheets, tools, and exercises that are best completed in small groups with your leaders and team members. If you should decide you need some extra support and accountability to implement this process, we offer coaching and consulting services to help you transform your firm much faster.

The rewards for this type of transformation are huge! This new paradigm can elevate your firm into the top tier in your industry. If you want to grow, make more money, enjoy your work more and make clients pursue you instead of the other way around, you will gain the strategy, specific steps and language skills to accomplish this and more.

Before you get started, I recommend taking a few minutes to score your firm's current value culture using our proprietary Value Quotient (VQ) Assessment (go to www.aecbusiness.com/RAISEYourValue/VQ or scan the QR Code below). This quick assessment will show you where you are strong and weak in relation to selling on value rather than price. Please send this link to others in your firm and see if they agree. Your goal after reading and applying the lessons of this book will be to increase your VQ so your entire firm culture is focused on value.

Take the VQ Assessment

With an open mind and commitment to improve, you will see remarkable results. I want to hear about your successes and even your challenges. Do not hesitate to reach out to me by email at jjewell@aecbusiness.com and connect with me on LinkedIn at https://www.linkedin.com/in/junejewell/

All of the tools, worksheets, and other resources discussed in this book are available at
www.aecbusiness.com/RAISEYourValue/Resources

Get Your Resources

CHAPTER 1

Ten Principles to RAISE Your Value

"When you undervalue what you do, the world will undervalue who you are."

— *Oprah Winfrey*

Raising your value in the minds of your clients, employees, and the rest of the world will transform your firm. You will win more work, more easily and at higher fees. You will get rid of clients that do not appreciate you, and your employees will be happier. But it cannot be accomplished with the same business practices, language, behaviors, and mindset that you have been operating with. Together we will discover what makes your firm unique and special. We will uncover your hidden value that sets you apart from your competition and will enable you to easily differentiate. The hidden value that you have always had but have not been able to leverage – until now.

There are ten key principles that you must understand and incorporate into your firm's culture and business practices that will radically alter how you market and go after business. These ten principles will change the behavior of your staff, build confidence in your seller-doers, and give your marketing team a new set of exciting messages to disseminate.

Your firm's focus on value can be calculated using an exclusive formula I have devised called the Value Quotient (VQ).

Just like you have an Intelligence Quotient (IQ) and Emotional Quotient (EQ), you can now measure your firm's Value Quotient (VQ). It is made up of five factors that when scored with our VQ Assessment, will help you understand the level to which you offer unique value, are perceived by your markets, and embrace your value as a firm. Your firm may need to calculate more than one VQ - one for each of the different business units or markets you specialize in. Go to www.aecbusiness.com/RAISEYourValue/VQ or scan the QR code below to start your assessment.

Take the VQ Assessment

By incorporating these ten principles into your firm's processes, you will create the Winning Advantage that will enable you to charge higher fees and elevate your firm to the top of your niche. We will cover these ten principles in much more detail throughout this book. Here is your introduction to the ten principles that will enable you to truly design a Winning Advantage:

1. Reframe the Meaning of Sales

Your seller-doers are not salespeople. They view sales as a distasteful responsibility that they would rather avoid. But you can reframe the meaning of sales so that it is viewed as a positive and enjoyable part of their jobs. Most A&E professionals are creative problem solvers.

They love a good challenge. By reframing sales as the first phase of the project, they can view sales as a challenge to find a solution that will give your clients exactly what they want.

When seller-doers view sales as helping the client succeed rather than trying to win, everyone benefits, and they enjoy the sales process much more.

2. Commoditization of A&E Services – Stop Self-Sabotaging

No A&E professional wants to become a commodity – viewed as the same as everyone else. When two or more firms appear to be the same, price becomes the key differentiating factor.

A&E services have become commoditized due to heavy competition, fee pressure, and self-sabotaging behaviors motivated by negative, self-limiting beliefs. These negative beliefs show up in countless ways including:

- Going after every client and project that comes along
- Lowering fee estimates to get work
- Discounting rates
- Not asking for change orders
- Giving away services for free / over-delivering
- Taking loss leaders (projects with very low or no profit)
- Being afraid to challenge clients when needed
- Failing to articulate your firm's benefits and value
- Ignoring the scope and budget on their projects

Fear of losing, fear of upsetting clients, even fear of being "too expensive" are causing your firm to lose out on higher fees, change orders, and upsells. Together we will stare down these self-limiting beliefs and expose them for what they are: FEAR – False Expectations Appearing Real.

3. Not All Clients Are Good Clients

In my first book, *Find the Lost Dollars: 6 Steps to Increase Profits in Architecture, Engineering and Environmental Firms*, I expose the ten Culture Traps that hold firms back from being profitable. One of these Culture Traps – All Clients are Good Clients – explains why A&E firms often take clients that are not good for their firm.

Admit it – some of your clients are mean, unreasonable, overly demanding, do not treat your employees well and then don't pay you. Even worse – some are unprofitable. Even bad clients whose projects provide a decent profit will suck the life out of your firm. They do not align with your values or take your advice and make your life a never-ending nightmare.

I will show you why you need to fire those clients and establish standards to drive future project and client selection. You can't be value driven and then work with clients you don't like. Once you have fully embraced this concept, your work and business will be much more enjoyable and successful.

4. The 80/20 Principle

The 80/20 Principle (also known as the Pareto Principle) is probably familiar to you, but you may not be leveraging it to your full advantage. According to the principle, when evaluating almost every area of business and life, we see that 80% of the results are derived from 20% of the efforts.

In business, this means that 80% of profits come from 20% of clients. Being able to analyze clients against the 80/20 rule, we can devise a better strategy that will yield more profitable and satisfying clients.

In Chapter 4 we will give some examples of how to apply the 80/20 rule to find and attain more of your ideal clients.

5. Defining Your Ideal Client

We all wish that all our clients could be more like our favorite client. The premise of this book is that this is possible. By defining what an ideal client is for your firm and developing a strategy to get more of them, you can eliminate working with undesirable clients.

Just as we must know the type of clients we want to work with, we must also know what types of clients we don't want to work with. The 80/20 Principle helps us with this too – 80% of your problems come from 20% of your clients. Having too many of these types of clients can ruin your culture and cause employees to leave. There is no reason to continue working with clients you don't love and that don't love you.

We will look at how to define your ideal client as well as "bad" clients. We will explore how to know quickly in your initial sales process, how to uncover their true motives to qualify or disqualify them before wasting too much time.

6. Five Ways to Differentiate

There are five ways to differentiate from your competition:

- Price
- Brand / Reputation
- Technology
- Service / Team
- Process

Every other method of differentiation is a variation of one of these 5. You may need to employ two or more of these methods to develop your Winning Advantage. You may need to use all five.

We will explore multiple ideas for differentiating using these five strategies. You may realize that you have been using the wrong method for years.

Each of these has pros and cons. As we are uncovering your hidden value and developing the tools to design your Winning Advantage, we will address each of them as part of formulating your strategy.

7. Your Winning Advantage – Unique Value Proposition (UVP) and Proprietary Process

To design your Winning Advantage, you will need to do some deep work to discover where you are different, better and add more value to clients. Through that process, and the exercises we will do as part of the 5- Step RAISE Your Value Formula, we will develop your Unique Value Proposition (UVP) and your Proprietary Process.

Your UVP will be your short "elevator pitch" that clearly describes why you are better, and why your ideal client should hire you instead of a competitor.

Your Proprietary Process will be a unique process and set of benefits that you will develop that no other firm has. This process will be described in the form of a unique acronym that represents your true value, and a graphic image, and when combined with your UVP, will form the foundation of your Winning Advantage.

8. Strategy and Your Values

Every firm needs a strategy to guide their growth. Your values should define your strategy – what you care about and how you intend to show up to clients, employees, and the world.

Unfortunately, I have found in my work that many A&E firms do not have a strategic plan, and their values are words on their web site and not principles that drive behavior.

Developing a value-driven strategic plan will help elevate your culture and employee retention and performance. We will look at the tenets of a good strategy and how it will help you leverage your Winning Advantage. If you already have a strategic plan, we will explore how to refine it to make it more value driven.

9. Strategic Pricing

A&E firms basically all price the same. Most firms use a combination of lump sum, hourly/T&M or Cost-Plus contractual arrangements to estimate fees and bill clients.

We will examine some strategic pricing methods used by other types of businesses and service providers that can be used to differentiate. Differentiating on price does not just mean that you have a higher or lower price. It can also single out your proposal by presenting pricing formats that clients have never seen before.

I will show you unique ways to upsell, cross-sell, and increase your contract value by introducing options that clients had not previously considered. I know you are thinking this is impossible, but it isn't. Depending on the client, type of project and service, pricing creatively can change the dynamics involved in your clients' decision- making process.

10. 5-Step RAISE Your Value Formula

Embracing and incorporating the nine principles above will enable you to differentiate your firm in remarkable ways. Finally, by implementing the 5-Step RAISE Your Value Formula in your firm, you will have a clear roadmap on how to uncover your unique hidden value, design your Winning Advantage, and leverage it in the marketplace to get better clients, higher fees and happier employees.

As seen in the figure below, the five steps are to RATE your current clients and develop your ideal client criteria, ASSESS your pricing, marketing, sales process and project financials, INVESTIGATE your unique value and create your Winning Advantage, STRATEGIZE how you want to leverage your unique value, and EXECUTE on your new strategic plan.

In Chapter 10 we will go through this process in detail. For now, trust that you can do this. Along the way, you will be given many self-explanatory tools to ensure you can be successful.

5-STEP RAISE YOUR VALUE FORMULA

Uncover Hidden Value, Design a Winning Advantage and Charge More

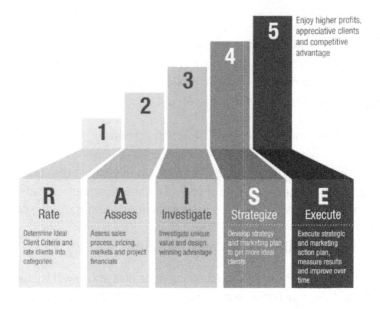

So, let's get started learning and adopting these 10 key principles to help your firm design your unique Winning Advantage!

CHAPTER 2

What Is Sales?

"Selling is something we do for our clients - not to our clients."

- Zig Ziglar

In every sales situation, there is a buyer and a seller. The buyer of A&E services is there for a reason. There is an outcome they need, and they are looking for the right solution. If your service is a commodity or even perceived as a commodity, they will focus on price. If your service is specialized, in high demand, has a reputation for being the best, and delivers the superior results you promise, then price becomes much less important.

But what if the seller can become the buyer? What if the seller gets to choose which clients they want and which ones to walk away from? What if the clients you choose to work with truly value the same things you do in terms of quality, reliability, timeline, and outcomes? Then the value the buyer offers to the seller in the form of compensation matches the high value the service provider is promising. In this case, the primary purpose of sales changes from merely trying to win, to deciding if we can be successful with the client.

Dan Sullivan, best-selling author and founder of Strategic Coach, advises that in our business and personal lives we should strive to always be the buyer:

"A seller is someone who can get rejected. A buyer is the one who does the rejecting. A buyer knows exactly what and who they're looking for. You want to be in a position where you're the one choosing an opportunity or relationship. You want to be the one who sets the standards.

Going from having a seller mindset to a buyer mindset is like suddenly being able to see an abundance of rewards and all the opportunities that are out there, where before there was scarcity."

Unfortunately, sales have gotten a bad rap. The image (popularized by television) of a sleazy used car salesperson lying to unsuspecting customers and "pulling a fast one" is engrained in all of us from a young age. For many professionals, sales is a dirty word.

But the car would never get sold and the car dealer would never be in business if it was not for the salesperson. As a customer, how would we understand the features of the car, differentiate it from other similar models, and ultimately, decide whether to buy it, or not?

Reframing the Meaning of Sales

The problem is that we do not have a framework for viewing sales properly. In selling design services, the sales process should be educational, both for the buyer and the seller. Michael T. Buell, AIA, FSMPS, National Strategist at HNTB gives this advice:

"What impacts your number of project opportunities and pursuit hit rates more than anything is a consistent focus on helping, not selling to, your clients. "HELP, DON'T SELL!" signs should be displayed throughout your office."

The buyer does not usually know how to buy what we are offering. It is our job to educate them. The salesperson, or in your case the seller-doer - technical professionals with sales responsibilities - does not know what the client really wants and what their expectations around scope, schedule, budget, and final deliverables really look like. It is your job to uncover this in sales conversations.

Sales activities are just the first phase of the project. Yes, we do not get paid for this work, but it is just as important as the other "billable" phases of the project. Sales is essential to uncovering potential clients' expectations, requirements, and success factors and determining if we can be successful completing their project, at a desired profit. It is also critical to deciding if we want to continue to pursue the project or walk away and free up our resources to work on better projects with better clients.

As the front end of the project, your sales process should help you:

- Qualify or disqualify the client or project
- Understand the client's values, requirements and expectations
- Get to know the client better
- Gain deep insight into the client's goals and expected outcomes
- Confirm how they will measure success
- Establish a partnership
- Develop a scope and estimate that truly matches what your client wants and needs
- Present a proposal that shows your true value

Your initial discussions should help you accomplish the following:

- Decide if you can fulfill client needs regarding terms of schedule, qualifications and resources
- Collect as much data as possible about the requirements for the project so you can develop an excellent scope and fee estimate
- Determine if the client's values align with your firm's values and strategic goals
- Understand the client's financial expectations and whether the project will meet your profit goals
- Ideally, establish a rapport between yourself and the client

It is not just the client who should decide whether your firm should move forward with the project. *You* should also be selective about which projects you take or walk away from. We will cover this in more detail in Chapter 5 when we discuss the Go/No-Go process and how it fits into your sales process.

It's the Client's Money

Clients either consider your services an expense or an investment. When they view you as an expense, their goal is to save money and spend as little as possible. When they view you as an investment, they realize the true cost is not what they pay you, but in whether they get the outcome they want and need.

Another important perspective to help reframe your view of sales is that ultimately, it's the client's money – not yours. Part of raising your value is realizing that true value is to help your client control their costs and get a return on investment (ROI) from their project. This is something many consultants don't focus on but can be a huge differentiator.

For example, as an architect, your cost to design a building is usually defined as your design fees, but as an experienced designer, you know that the true cost to the client is in the final construction, sustainability and energy costs, maintenance costs, and long-term performance of the building as well as many other aesthetic and functional factors.

Your role in the sales process is to educate the client about all the future costs that you are going to save them, as well as all the important factors and pitfalls they may not know to consider. This is where your true value and differentiation occurs.

How Sales Affects Your Success

A big part of my success as a business consultant is because of my focus on sales effectiveness. In my systems consulting and training businesses, we developed an elaborate sales process that ensured the success of every project. Every time we encountered a problem on a project, we analyzed how it could have been prevented and changed our sales process to ensure it would never happen again. We also got really good about setting expectations about what could go wrong, and what types of issues could cause the project to go over budget. We even put all of this into an appendix in our proposals and reviewed it with clients before they signed the contract.

Our clients appreciated the education and the fact that we were going the extra mile to make them successful. It is not enough to win the sale. Your sales process should be the start of a genuine partnership that reassures the client you are working in their interest and that they will get what they paid for.

Sales are not effective just because you win the work. In fact, winning the work can be the worst outcome of a well- executed sales process. A poorly run sales process—one that fails to vet clients properly and is focused exclusively on closing the deal—will cost your firm money, clients, and worse, talented employees. By failing to select the right clients and projects, you jeopardize the future growth and reputation of your firm. Your primary purpose in the sales process is to determine if a project is a good fit and collect all the information you need to properly develop the scope and budget. It is also critical to get to know your client and set appropriate expectations. Without this focus, you will get bad clients.

Bad clients divert focus and resources from good clients. They stress out your staff, demand too much, and create drama daily. Bad clients ask for too much, and then refuse to pay on time, or at all. Bad clients refuse to take your advice, thinking they know it all. They are not appreciative and treat you like a vendor instead of a valued advisor.

Most professionals go into a short-list interview thinking *they* are the ones being interviewed. Just as much scrutiny should be put into interviewing the client to determine if you should select them.

If you take nothing else away from this book, it should be that how you sell and select clients is more important than any other factor in determining how successful your firm is and how happy your employees are. Instead of selling on price, you can establish a sales process based on demonstrating the unique value you bring to your ideal client. Later we will explore the specific steps to help you implement a value-based sales process and educate your team to share your Winning Advantage.

Why Seller-Doers Hate Sales

Many A&E firms do not have professional sales teams. Sales are managed by firm principals and seller-doers – technical professionals that are promoted into project management roles and required to sell as part of their many responsibilities. Compared to running the technical aspect of a project, sales are often viewed by seller-doers as daunting and out of their wheelhouse. They may believe they are terrible at sales and often wonder why firm leaders are asking them to do something they are not good at or trained to do.

Even those firms that have developed excellent sales processes struggle to consistently hold seller-doers accountable for results. Incentive plans and heavy focus on business development and interview tactics will help, but most seller-doers still struggle to become proficient at sales. Jim Rogers, founder of Seller Doer Academy (http://sellerdoeracademy.com/) is the author of the brilliant book *Becoming a Seller-Doer,* specifically written for the A&E professional required to assist with generating sales revenue. Jim defines a seller-doer as a "billable professional who takes purposeful action to help generate revenue for their firm." Jim provides this advice to A&E firm leaders about how to motivate seller-doers despite their fears and find more creative ways to reward them for sales success:

"Inertia is the biggest enemy of the seller-doer. Inertia results from their dread of doing something they're uncomfortable with. Dread leads technical professionals and project managers to hide behind the work that they're most comfortable with—client delivery.

Great leaders create environments that help employees overcome dread. Begin by supplying training and job assignments with on-the-job coaching and permit them to fail as an essential part of the learning process.

Another way to lead change is to disassociate success at sales from climbing the corporate ladder—that is, advancing in rank. Instead of relying on the carrot of career advancement, make it about taking command of their careers and reaping other rewards. Think beyond monetary rewards and employ a range of recognition tactics such as incremental progressions in titles, access to training, public praise, job rotation, a plumb assignment, or permission to say no to being assigned to a ho-hum project."

The key to seller-doer success lies in reframing the meaning of sales to your seller-doers. When you learn to reframe the concept of sales as the *first phase of the project* and their role as problem solver, educator, and guardian of the client's project success, selling becomes a much more enjoyable responsibility.

Most seller-doers have not been trained to talk about value. Through the work you will do in this book and accompanying workshops, anyone required to sell will learn the secrets to having solid business conversations about results, value, and outcomes instead of technical aspects and deliverables. When they learn the RAISE Your Value techniques, language skills, and approach, your seller- doers will have confidence having difficult conversations and become the valued advisors that will differentiate your firm from your competitors.

Helping Seller-Doers Succeed

Taking technical professionals and turning them into salespeople is difficult at best. Some will refuse. Others will be ineffective. It is imperative that you give them every chance for success by offering sales training, role-playing, scripts, elevator speeches, and other tools. If you leave it up to them to figure it out alone, they will fail miserably.

Frank Lippert, FSMPS, CPSM, Principal, GO Strategies, LLC, has this advice for any firm trying to help introverted seller-doers to be successful:

> *"Not all business development needs to be shaking hands and making killer deals. Sometimes the simplest actions can bring awareness to expertise and prompt a client to reach out to you.*
>
> *Years ago, when blogging was newer, I worked with a seller-doer who was more introverted than most. "I really hate events. My palms sweat. I can't get my words out. I want to throw up... it's a lot of anxiety," he told me. Playing to his strengths, I recognized that he was an environmental expert really focused on sea-level rise and its impacts on endangered species, an important concern for our clients. He was also tech-savvy and an excellent, concise writer.*
>
> *So, we started a strategy where he looked over a series of different clients' blogs routinely. When appropriate, he posted short, intelligent responses that demonstrated his knowledge. He always ended each post with his name, email, and phone number. He was diligent about this, documenting in a spreadsheet every response. After more than three months, I vividly remember him running down the hall to my office to tell me when someone had*

responded. "The client just called and we're meeting next week!" he said, out of breath.

Four things are key here: (1) play to people's strengths not their weakness, (2) have a strategy for behind-the-scenes efforts like this, (3) have good, intelligent, meaningful (and brief) responses, and (4) stick with the plan (it took three months to see a return, it could take longer).

Eventually my seller-doer met with the client and was awarded a small foot-in-the-door, direct-appoint contract. He delivered exceptionally well on (a critical step in winning work) and today has leveraged it into multiple awards. He is still uncomfortable at client events, but he's built relationships through delivering good work and has not thrown up lately."

With help, your seller doers can learn to be successful, confident leaders who bring valuable work in the door.

CHAPTER 3

Commoditization of A&E Services – Stop Sabotaging Your Success

"Commoditization is the process of continually making something the same and undifferentiated. When things become undifferentiated, they become cheap."

- Gabe Lett, FSMPS, CPSM, LPC, Author, The AEC Professionals Guidebook, (https://www.theaecguide.com/)

When there is no perceived difference between you and your competitors, your services become commoditized – presumed to be the same – and price becomes the key, if not the only, factor in selection.

The Great Recession of 2008-2011 caused a lot of A&E firms to lower their prices to compete. Many bad habits were created during this time, including lowering prices below break-even levels just to get a foot in the door with a new client or keep staff utilized to avoid layoffs.

After the recession ended and demand for design services started to increase, these bad habits often persisted. Because price had been such a crucial factor in winning work during the recession, many A&E firms continued to accept unprofitable work, or work with low profit margins. Unfortunately, these damaging habits still exist! Even when salaries and business overhead costs are rising and design services are in demand, firms are still unwisely competing on price and lowering fees to win.

If you are in an industry or market that has become commoditized, it is usually because of one of the following reasons:

- Failure to differentiate based on value
- Fear of failure/losing
- Not believing you are better than competitors
- Lack of financial literacy
- Focus on the wrong priorities
- Pursuit of revenue instead of profit
- No strategy or poorly implemented strategy
- Feeling shame for charging clients for passion projects
- Self-limiting beliefs (see below)

Chad Clinehans, P.E., CEO of Zweig Group, Fayetteville, AR believes that professionals are inflicting pain on themselves with their commoditizing behaviors:

> *"Commoditization is somewhat of a self-fulfilling prophecy. Leaders must understand that if they continue to say the same thing everyone else is saying, not work hard to select the right clients, and continue working for clients where they can't be profitable, they commoditize themselves.*
>
> *There is tremendous opportunity to create unique and compelling brands in this industry where you can attract the best people and clients. That's where you get pricing power – through strong brands and brand loyalty from an ideal target market."*

How Self-Limiting Beliefs Sabotage Sales

As Brian Tracy, public speaker and author, says, *"You begin to fly when you let go of self-limiting beliefs and allow your mind and aspirations to rise to greater heights."* A&E firms should take this advice to heart.

One of the reasons consultants find themselves commoditized and competing on price is because of their self-limiting beliefs. Everyone has self-limiting beliefs that affect the success of their relationships, work effectiveness, and sales results. By becoming more aware of your own self-limiting beliefs, and those of the people you lead, you can work to eliminate them and transform every aspect of your life to have greater success.

A self-limiting belief is a belief that you hold to be true even though it is not. These beliefs often start in childhood and become engrained in our thought patterns like bad habits. A self-limiting belief may be about money, relationships, how things work in the world, or even about our own competence.

These beliefs affect how we operate at work and can deter our success. In a sales situation, or development of a client relationship, they can sabotage our growth. Self-limiting beliefs show up the most when we are in perceived difficult conversations, negotiations, and disputes. They make us undervalue our own capabilities.

In typical sales training courses, self-limiting beliefs are addressed and hopefully dispelled. But most seller-doers never get sales training and are unaware these beliefs are causing them to act against their own best interest.

Some examples of common self-limiting beliefs include:

- The client will never pay that much
- We are no better than other (fill in the blank – engineers, architects, consultants)
- $5,000 is a lot of money
- Clients are hard to get
- The client will be mad if I ask them to pay the bill
- I will annoy the client if I ask too many questions
- I must prove I am better than the competition
- The client will never hire us over the incumbent
- All clients want low prices
- I am terrible at sales
- The client does not trust "salespeople"
- I am too young/old to do this
- Buyers have all the power
- I am not good at this
- I am not good enough

This is not a comprehensive list. You may have other beliefs that are limiting your ability to get paid what you are worth.

You can see that these types of beliefs may cause someone in a sales conversation or discussion about money to avoid a dispute or perceived challenge. Every day I see A&E professionals make bad decisions because they believe a client will not pay more or will be upset if they increase their prices. I hear excuses such as:

- The market won't bear higher rates
- They will just go and hire someone else
- I am afraid we will lose
- The client says we are "nickel and diming" them
- I do not want to lose our best client (hint – they aren't your best client if they won't pay more to get you on their team)
- If I ask the client for a change order, they will get mad

The real danger is that these beliefs are passed down unknowingly from leaders to their employees and become part of the culture. Beliefs like "the client will not pay that much," or "there are other (fill in the blanks that can do this as well as we can for a lower price" become roadblocks to growth and profitability.

My colleague, Kevin Sombart, Sr. Advisor at AEC Business Solutions is constantly challenged with helping clients get past their limiting beliefs:

> *"I work with dozens of architectural and engineering firms and almost all have one thing in common; they are uncomfortable asking a client for money. You must first truly believe the services you provide have substantial value to your clients and really know what that value is. Once you convince yourself and your employees of that, you must be willing to ask your clients to pay you for that value. Failing to make that ask simply diminishes your value to your clients and to your employees."*

Years ago, I worked with a 50-person MEP engineering firm that had not raised their fees in five years. A few of their principals understood their financial situation and wanted to increase billing rates. Several others were adamant that if they did increase their rates, they would lose clients. This battle went on over the course of a year during which they did nothing. In that time, they only had a 6% profit. The leadership team finally agreed to raise rates and met with each of their key clients to explain why it was necessary. Not one client objected to the price increase. In the following year they doubled their profit to 12%. If they had raised their prices a year earlier, they would have made over $500,000 more. That profit could have helped to fuel growth, hire new project managers, upgrade their marketing and technology, and give their staff bonuses.

Every day you wait to raise your fees, you lose revenues you can't get back. These self-inflicted wounds perpetuate unless challenged. The first step to eliminate the fear and related behaviors is to become aware of them when they happen, identifying the ones that have the biggest power over you, and finding methods to overcome them.

In Chapter 7 we will explore ways you can build confidence selling and talking about money, so your fears and self-limiting beliefs do not have such a negative impact. It is possible to replace your self-limiting beliefs with new beliefs that recognize and appreciate your true value. Next time you are in a situation with a client and recognize limiting beliefs occurring, here are steps you can take to overcome their impact:

- Identify the self-limiting beliefs that are having the biggest impact on your performance and behavior and where they show up.

- Write down all the reasons your self-limiting beliefs are not true. For example, if you believe your competitors are just as competent as you are, write down all the factors that make you better than other consultants in your industry.

- Consider the worst-case scenario and learn to be okay when a client does not like your position. Try to get comfortable with any outcome and rehearse responses to the different scenarios so you feel more prepared.

- Embrace new beliefs that are the opposite of the limiting beliefs. For example, if you believe clients will get angry if you ask for a change order, create an alternative belief that says that the extra services you are providing have greater value to the client than what you are charging them.

By realizing that limiting beliefs are false, you can start to have more control over your client interactions and guide them to a more favorable outcome. This story was conveyed to me by Roman Kmenta (https://www.romankmenta.com/, international keynote speaker, author, sales training expert, and business coach:

> *"In my first year as an independent sales trainer, I was in a sales interview with a potential client. After we talked, the question of price inevitably came up. I presented it as professionally as I could at the time.*
>
> *While insecurities that sellers have about their price are often obvious, I quoted my prices cleanly and confidently. But that alone does not mean the customer won't object. And it did come in the form of, "You're pretty high-priced."*
>
> *Young and still relatively inexperienced in this business, I responded without even a second's hesitation. "Yes, but for that you also have top quality .... blah blah ..." I began to justify myself and explain to my customer why the price was so high. I made the mistake that many salespeople and businesspeople make every day. I brought up arguments to justify the high price.*
>
> *It is not wrong or bad to use such arguments in a sales pitch, the question is when and how. The same statements about quality are perfectly fine in the presentation of a product or service. But in response to a price objection, they easily sound like a justification, or even an excuse, for the fact that the price is as high as it is. And a seller should never apologize for their price. It also depends on the tone with which these arguments are made. The line between a justification and a clean benefit argument is a very thin one.*

After about a minute, she cleverly uses a small pause in speech between my justifications and interrupts me. "That doesn't mean we wouldn't hire you because of that," she says. I felt like I had been slapped in the face, a slap that shook me awake and snapped me out of my rut of justifications. I tried not to let on.

"No, it doesn't mean that at all," I thought. The realization came late, but it did come. How often do we buy something we think is high-priced, TOO expensive even, something beyond our budget? I do, all the time. So why should our customers be any different? Customers buy despite the high price when the value the sellers offer exceeds the price.

In some cases, like the luxury goods market, for example, they even buy BECAUSE OF the high price. A bargain is what we all want, but who (if he or she can afford it) wants something CHEAP? What company wants to boast that it has bought the CHEAPEST consultant they could get? Ultimately, there is nothing that is too expensive. A lot of things are just not worth enough.

And yes, the client hired me several times over the course of a few years. Fortunately, even with (serious) mistakes, selling works out in some cases."

Fast/Good/Cheap – You Can Only Have Two

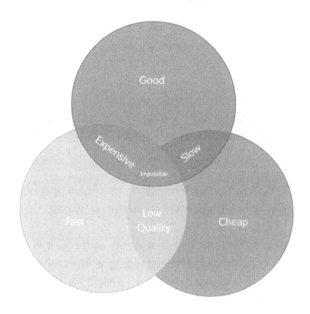

There is an old paradigm that rings true with professional services: there is good, fast, and cheap – but you can only have two. Part of the challenge of effective pricing and negotiation for services is balancing client requirements and expectations for schedule, quality and budget. Unless you are willing to operate at a loss or low profit margins, it is impossible to deliver your highest quality, as fast as possible. Realistically, we would not want to do this even if we could.

Unless you want to be the low-cost vendor in your industry, and consistently compete on price, you will want to ensure you can deliver high quality as quickly as possible. This will require that your prices reflect this level of quality and speed, and clients who value quality and fast turnaround will be willing to pay extra to get it.

When developing your strategic plan, it is important to decide what you want to be known for. If high quality is extremely important to your brand and reputation, you will want to be on the high end of the price spectrum. This will require targeting a certain clientele that can afford this level of quality.

If a client requires fast turnaround, you may have to shuffle resources, pull people off other projects and realign schedules for other clients. If you deliver high quality and fast turnaround, clients should pay a premium.

If a client has a low budget, something must give. It is not financially viable to offer your highest-level service at a low cost.

When confronted with a client that wants all three, it is important to have a value conversation. Understanding what is most important to the client will enable you to determine if a client aligns with your values and is a client worth keeping.

Having the Fast/Good/Cheap conversation early in the sales process will enable you to avoid problems later and, in some cases walk away when client expectations are not realistic. Unfortunately, most of your employees are more focused on technical excellence and keeping clients happy. They want to deliver good, fast and cheap, and don't understand that delivering all three is a recipe for financial disaster for your firm.

Revisiting the Culture Traps

In my book, Find the Lost Dollar: 6 Steps to Increase Profits in Architecture, Engineering and Environmental Firms, I introduced 10 Culture Traps. These are the commonly held beliefs, myths and assumptions that cause professional consultants to get bad clients, leave money on the table and not optimally run their businesses.

When selling your services, three of these traps often influence the behavior of your leaders and managers:

Trap # 2 – Keep the Client Happy at All Costs

In your staff's desire to keep clients happy, they often give away the farm (firm. They over-deliver, under charge and avoid conflict. Best business practices like refusing to start a project without a contract, asking for a change order, or calling about a past due invoice are avoided because of a fear of conflict – and upsetting a client.

Trap # 4 – All Clients Are Good Clients

Professionals often believe that good clients are hard to find so they put up with poor behavior from bad clients. They treat all clients the same, even if some of them treat our staff badly, are overly demanding, and then don't pay!

Trap #7 – Our Clients Don't Want us to Make a Profit

This myth causes your staff to lower fees to compete. They have been beaten down in the past and believe that all clients care about is the cost.

By eliminating these three traps from our employees' mindsets, we can improve their outlook and teach them to sell on value.

Business Acumen and Performance

Another root cause of commoditizing behavior is a lack of understanding about business. Many professionals tune out leadership discussions about profit and finances, believing it does not affect them.

My experience working with over 1,000 technical professionals since 2014 in the Find the Lost Dollars business and financial management training program is employees radically change their viewpoint towards financial matters such as pricing and fees when exposed to the "why" behind the importance of making a profit.

When they understand how the bottom line affects them personally and can see a correlation between the firm's financial success and their own, they behave differently and approach rate changes and discussions about money more positively.

Lee James, CPA, CBI, CMC, founder of Lee James & Associates, Inc. explains the inevitable result of valuing your technical work over your business results:

> "A&E professionals do not believe in their business like they believe in their technical practice. This needs to change; and become a both/and instead of an either/or. The firms that make this a both/and are consistently upper quartile performers; and those that are especially poor at this are consistently lower quartile firms."

In 2017 I worked with Russ Sanford, FSPMS, CPSM, Senior Vice President and Chief Growth Officer at Kleinschmidt, who has seen how a lack of business training causes their clients to view technical professionals as a commodity:

> "As an engineer by education who's grown to become the chief growth officer of a 220+ person engineering and environmental consulting firm, it frustrates me to see technical professionals undervalue their services. One of the reasons I believe this happens is that technical staff do not learn business principles and business skills in college. When they learn that a business should be designed to be effective, efficient, and profitable, then they begin to understand that improving their business begins with developing large, repeat clients who value the services

they provide. Companies can do this by building strong client relationships and becoming the clients' trusted advisor.

Unfortunately, too many firms in our industry feel that clients only care about low price and are afraid to pick up the phone and ask questions. As a result, our clients begin to look at our whole industry with a commoditization mindset and we all suffer! Building loyal client relationships and understanding what they value is how we can all overcome this challenge. It does take discipline though. Firms need to understand the purpose behind creating strategic plans and developing proactive marketing and business development plans. The ones that don't value and invest in their growth will ultimately disappear."

Overcoming the Fear of Change – The Great Benefits that Await

While it is not easy to implement a new strategy to move from commodity to preferred and high-priced service provider, it can be done by following the 5-Step RAISE Your Value formula outlined in Chapter 10. Making these changes will take commitment, time, effort, and most importantly, changing your mindset. Knowing and communicating your true value is the key to transforming your firm from a commodity to the most valued firm in your market.

I have seen many firms over the years that wanted to make this change but could not get past their fear of changing and the comfort of staying the same. Some firms have maintained the same rates for five or more years, too scared of losing clients to increase prices. But the firms that have risen above their fear, and made the decision to change, have seen transformational, explosive results in just a couple years.

When facilitating a leadership training program in 2017 with Kleinschmidt, a growing engineering and environmental firm headquartered in Maine, we focused on a key initiative to rate their clients, identify their ideal client goals, and implement a client selection strategy and price increases based on winning with clients that appreciated their value.

We also analyzed their project profitability and discovered their lump sum projects were more profitable than their hourly projects. As Jon Christensen, CEO of Kleinschmidt, explains, record growth and profits occurred following implementation of this combined strategy:

> *"Emerging from the Great Recession, we were blessed with significant workload, especially a few very large projects, which surprisingly enabled us to grow through the economic challenges that plagued so many firms in our industry. This also enabled us to position Kleinschmidt for success through client relationships.*
>
> *Delivering relationship-based services has just a few tenets. First, and foremost, we develop loyal relationships with clients who appreciate our work. We emphatically focus on delivering value, by learning the client's interests and needs and strategizing how to help them succeed. We charge for the value we add with rates that are more competitive with big companies and by using lump sum projects where it makes sense for us and our clients (a surprising number of clients prefer price predictability above minimum price, we've found).*
>
> *For our second tenet, we focus on delivering innovative technical excellence. Innovating our services delivers better client-focused solutions faster and less expensively. This innovation encourages clients to move our team forward in the project life cycle and bring us their problems*

and challenges, rather than asking us to bid on the solutions that they develop.

Several clients even work with us to strategically prioritize their portfolio-wide needs. As an additional benefit, we have significantly improved staff engagement as they embrace our investment in innovation.

The final tenet of our relationship-driven model relates to active ongoing analysis of clients. Based on our work with June Jewell in the Find the Lost Dollars training, we developed a simple rating system. This approach allowed us to focus more of our energy and time on clients with whom we enjoyed a strong working relationship, and to minimize/eliminate the distraction of continuing our efforts with low-price selectors.

Our clients today must fit into one of these categories:

__FOUNDATIONAL CLIENTS__ – Clients we are highly engaged with at multiple levels and across multiple disciplines. Bidding is sole source or moderately competitive (accounting for some companies who "must obtain multiple quotes" from no more than 3 competitors).

__LOYAL CLIENTS__ – Clients who preferentially select us when their purchasing rules allow. Their selection criteria must be primarily driven by quality and creativity/applicability of approach, rather than price.

__DEVELOPMENTAL CLIENTS__ – Clients who may become Foundational or Loyal. This is our pipeline for future workload.

__OTHER__ – If a client does not fit this list, and their project is *not highly important to us for the opportunistic reasons noted below, we do not bid.*

OPPORTUNISTIC PROJECTS - *We do not rate "projects," only "clients". Occasionally, we will pursue projects that are very complicated, but within our skill sets, or that fit a strategic geographic or service need – in other words, places where we feel the odds of success are high or that are so important that we will determine how to win.*

Early after we made this change, we nervously informed several clients who frequently selected on price that we would no longer prepare competitive bids for them. While a few simply took us off their bidders list (we expected all to do this), several of these clients stated overtly that the quality of our products/services was so superior to what they got elsewhere that they wanted us to continue bidding their projects. To those clients, we said we would be happy to bid on sole-source work ONLY, and that we would not negotiate prices. We still work with some of those clients today. This is the most obvious example of how this can work... clearly, these clients wanted the value we provided, but they wanted it at a commodity price.

The unexpected benefit was that we began winning a far greater percentage of our moderately competitive proposals. Staff who previously churned out four to five proposals per week suddenly found themselves delivering one or two higher- quality proposals per week. They used the other "found time" to improve deliverables for existing clients or to perform other innovation or development projects that advanced our company goals, all of which led to improved win rates on future projects.

In short, the relationship-based approach creates a

synergistic circle of opportunity and reward. We serve our clients better, and they are more willing to pay us for that value and provide better project opportunities. We use the increased revenues to improve benefits and the project opportunities to provide an awesome technical and innovation experience, which gets employees more engaged and excited. Finally, engaged employees serve our clients much better, starting the cycle all over again!

After four years of this approach, we've accumulated some fantastic results. In the past 4 years, our multiplier has increased from below 3.0 to around 3.4. Our profitability, which was hovering around 8-10%, has increased to routinely come in at 15-20%. We achieved that increase at the same time we dramatically increased our employee training and development programs and our benefits package. We nearly doubled in size in the past four years from 120 to almost 220 today. While this included one acquisition of 25 people, the rest has occurred through organic growth."

This strategy can work for small, medium, and even large firms. Bob Kelleher, CEO of The Employee Engagement Group and former Chief Human Resources officer at AECOM, has been a part of many initiatives to increase revenues in his long career in the A&E industry. He recounts the benefits of focusing on raising prices as a strategy:

"In a 30-year career, though I've been part of countless 'Increase Utilization" task teams, I've never seen better tangible bottom line results until the time I participated on a "Getting Paid For Our Value" task team. Especially in these times, where there is an obvious supply and demand shift underway favoring higher pricing. It's simply economics 101."

With rising costs and aggressive growth goals, raising rates is critical to ensuring your business can thrive. Many firms wait too long or allow fear of losing clients keep them from moving forward with needed rate increases. When working with Hillmann Consulting, a 250+ employee environmental consulting firm headquartered in Union, NJ, I advised them to raise prices for many years. While some of their divisions had successfully raised prices, there was still some hesitation to raise rates across the board. With growing labor and overhead costs and ambitious goals for growth, they made the decision in 2022 to finally increase rates across the firm. Jacob Hillmann, Chief Strategy Officer, describes their decision to increase rates:

> *"Like many firms post-pandemic, Hillmann assessed employee engagement and salaries, escalating vendor costs, and revenue and profit goals. Hillmann, in alignment with our culture, absorbed any increase in the cost of health insurance and offered dental and vision benefits at no cost to employees. Additionally, we increased salaries across the board, helping us maintain our strong workforce and superior client service.*
>
> *It became apparent – we had to increase our rates not only to communicate value and appreciation to our expert talent, but to continue to utilize our quality laboratories and vendors, support our corporate initiatives, and donate 10% of our profits to charitable organizations.*
>
> *When we partner with our clients, our goal is their goal whether it's bringing tenants back to their buildings, responding to disasters, or managing developers' budgets. Our clients expect rapid response, quality work product, and expert consulting; the increase in rates enabled us to continue exceeding these expectations. Three months into raising our pricing, despite apprehension from some of our managers, we have received little to no negative feedback*

and certainly have not lost clients as a result."

It is common to be afraid to increase rates. We are all programmed to want to help our clients, and rate increases are viewed as hurting them. But raising prices actually help your clients by ensuring they will continue to receive your top-level service even when your own costs are rapidly rising.

Steve Gido, Principal, ROG Partners believes there are opportunities in the current environment to raise the value of your firm through differentiation:

> *"In my experience, the A/E industry needs to convey its value proposition of design and consulting solutions more effectively to clients and stakeholders. There are many opportunities for leaders to break out of the commoditization mindset driven by rampant competition and lack of confidence. From selecting the best clients, to smarter financial and project management, there is a path forward to higher multipliers and profitability."*

To be successful with the RAISE Your Value Formula, you are going to have to change the mindset of your team from fear to enthusiasm. Keep reading – I will show you exactly how to do this and guide you every step of the way.

CHAPTER 4

The 80/20 Rule and How it Affects Your Success

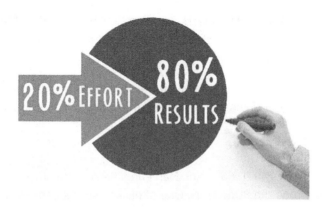

The Pareto Principle, also known as the 80/20 rule, is a well-known but little understood principle that, when applied, can help you learn what clients to target and what to offer them. It can also help you understand what selling activities are having the biggest impact, which services you offer make the biggest profits, and which employees contribute the most to your firm.

The 80/20 rule stipulates that 20% of effort generates 80% of results. This rule can be applied to everything in life. It is evident in both personal and business situations. In some cases, it may be more like 70/30 or 90/10. Looking at many different examples of the 80/20 rule, it can provide tremendous insight into trends, best practices and time management.

The 80/20 rule can provide so many insights into what is working and what is not including:

- Identify which types of clients are the most profitable. In many firms, 20% of clients account for 80% of profit.
- Discover which marketing efforts generate the most leads.
- Determine what to sell to your ideal clients.
- Learn which 20% of your employees generate 80% of your results.
- Uncover which types of projects are best for your firm.
- Determine which daily efforts are most effective and which ones to stop doing

By understanding how your efforts drive results, you can minimize activities that do not serve you and maximize activities that do.

The Power Curve

In his book, 80/20 Sales and Marketing, Perry S. Marshall teaches how to leverage the 80/20 rule. One of his key insights, the Power Curve, helps demonstrate the power of charting your clients to understand the small percentage that spend the most money with your firm. By taking the *20% of the 20%,* you can see in the figure below that up to 64% of your results come from 4% of your efforts/work/clients.

The best way to chart your results on the power curve is with profits. While it is important to understand the clients that have the most money to spend and give you the highest revenue, *profits* tell a better story.

Many leaders believe their best clients are the ones giving them the most work – or revenue. But in my extensive analysis of A&E firm profitability over many years, I have found high *revenue* clients are often the least *profitable*. In fact, clients that generated the highest revenue and were pampered the most can be the most demanding, the slowest payers, and the least appreciative. The following is an example of a power curve based on Perry Marshall's Power Curve in *80/20 Sales and Marketing*.

PROFIT POWER CURVE

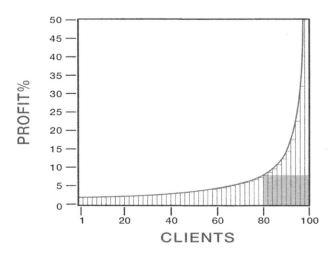

Figure 1

If you plot your "top" 100 clients on the X axis and profit percentage on the Y axis, you will see the 20% of clients providing 80% of your profit. Profit is a much better determination of client value than revenue.

If you use the 80/20 rule to analyze your clients, you will see your time is better spent pursuing specific types of clients. By understanding which types of clients, types of services, markets and geographies you are most successful, you can devise a strategy to pursue more of those types of clients. This insight can also save you from wasting time with clients that have no money to spend or are not profitable.

I also like to chart the revenue and profit on the same graph to understand which clients have the highest combination of revenue and profit. By creating a scatter chart using the average project revenue on the Y axis and the average project profit percentage on the X axis, you can chart your clients according to their relative value to each other. This approach enables you to value both revenue and profit when analyzing who your best clients really are.

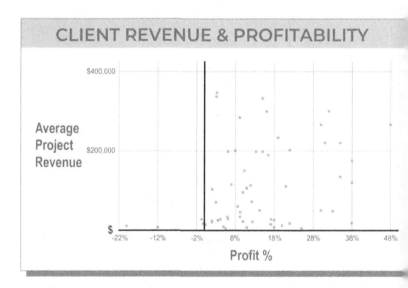

Not All Clients Want the Same Things

The 80/20 rule teaches us that our best clients do not value the same things as the clients that select on price. They value aspects of our services that the "cheap" clients don't. It is important to learn about your clients so you can offer exactly what they are looking for. The 80/20 Power Curve enables us to target those clients that are most financially valuable to our firm and reach out to them to learn more about what they value.

Unfortunately, many professionals have a boilerplate approach to their services. Proposals are often created from templates and rarely customized to consider differences in client preferences.

What is often overlooked are small differences that clients prefer. Below we will examine two examples of industries that have mastered the art of segregating clients and capitalizing on the 80/20 rule in creative ways.

The Airline Industry

The airline industry excels at figuring out how to get more revenue out of each customer. They have done this through extensive research and understanding of their customers. Each traveler has different preferences and is willing to spend more or less depending on what they value.

When I fly, my number one concern is having a non-stop flight. I have spent too many hours stranded or missing connections. I will only fly non-stop, and I am willing to pay more for a non- stop flight. Other people do not care about this. Their money is more valuable than their time.

I also have Platinum Status on United which gets me special treatment. I can board early, get free checked bags and free seat upgrades. I also have Club membership. Because I fly frequently, these perks make my travel more pleasant and predictable.

Here are some of the benefits most airlines charge more for:

- Non-stop versus stops
- Type of seat – cabin, extra legroom, etc.
- Checked bags

- Carry-on allowed
- Boarding order
- Food and drinks
- Wi-Fi
- Premium entertainment
- Time of flight
- Status
- Points earned per flight
- Club / Lounge Access

While each person is starting and ending in the same location (deliverable), the scope changes based on the passenger's preferences and what they are willing to pay.

First Class Cabin

Major League Baseball (MLB)

Another industry that is great at making money by adding extra benefits is major league sports. If you think about the Power Curve, in reviewing the expenditure of 100,000 fans for a game, there are huge gaps in amount spent per person. The person sitting in the nosebleed may spend 1/ 1000th of what a corporate suite holder would pay for a suite.

2019 Washington Nationals World Series Tickets

How Much Are Nationals 2019 World Series Tickets?

Secondary market Nationals World Series tickets are currently averaging $2,492 per seat. Get-in prices for the games at Nationals Park range from $544 for game 5, up to $1,279 for game 4 in DC. Below are average, get-in prices and ticket links for each game:

NATIONALS WORLD SERIES TICKET PRICES		
Game	Avg	Get-In Price
Game 3	$2,701	$1,125
Game 4	$2,665	$1,279
Game 5	$1,874	$544

Source: https://blog.ticketiq.com/blog/how-to-find-the-cheapest-world- series-tickets

MLB owners know that corporations will spend a lot to impress their clients. They have added many "VIP" extras to their offering including having luxury food and beverages, special events, access to the players, field, or dressing rooms after the game, etc.

During the 2019 World Series when "my" Washington Nationals (Nats) played against Houston in D.C., tickets in the regular seats ranged from $544 to $1,279. But people sitting in the suites paid $20,000 or more to have a small group of friends attend one of the three home games in luxury. The interesting statistic is that the prices in Houston were less than the prices in D.C. by between 25% to 40%.

This shows us that price is often very elastic based on what people care about and are willing/able to spend.

If they offered all seats at the same price, they would lose a lot of money. By understanding their big spending customers, they can come up with strategic pricing offers. While the profit per customer is much higher for these clients, there are fewer of them so they must make up the difference in volume. In Chapter 9 we will look at some ways we can apply strategic pricing to A&E services.

Knowing Your Clients: Defining Value

These examples show us that by using the 80/20 rule to figure out who our top spending and most profitable clients are, we can then devise a strategy to give them exactly what they want and potentially increase our revenues and prices.

To charge more for your services, you must know what your clients value. The biggest mistake a business can make is to assume clients will not pay more for preferred access, faster service, more frequent status updates, more detailed reporting or an upgraded experience. Some clients will even pay more to work with a firm that has an outstanding brand or reputation, spends money to entertain them, or that guarantees a certain result.

Most clients have had bad experiences before. They have been ripped off, tricked, disappointed, overcharged by, and frustrated with your competitors. They are savvy buyers and don't want to experience those feelings again. The clients that want excellent results are willing to pay for it.

Even *you* may not understand the real value you provide, and thus you aren't leveraging it as a Winning Advantage in your sales process. It often requires digging deep into your projects to uncover the money saved, an easier process, reduced stress, reduced risk, increased pleasure, and long-term value you add to clients.

The key to selling on value is simple – *determine what your ideal premier clients value and sell it to them.* This approach will provide your firm with a strong competitive advantage.

The only way to find out what your clients really want is to ask them. But this can be difficult if you are not prepared to offer more.

There are two key challenges to defining value:

1. Value is defined differently for different people. You must understand what your clients believe is valuable and ensure you can deliver it. It may or may not be what you think it is or should be.

2. Your competitors are all using the same words to tout the value they deliver. You must sound and BE different. Otherwise, your value promises sound like everyone else.

The solution to these challenges is to determine who your ideal client is and define what value is for them. Clients that value the long-term results of your efforts more than the short-term cost of your fees will resonate with your value promises. In the next chapter, we will dive into how to uncover the attributes of your ideal client so you can get more of them and reject clients who don't appreciate your unique value.

CHAPTER 5

Your Ideal Clients

Your ideal clients will bring you joy, fulfillment and profits.

There is an opportunity cost to your work. You only have so many resources to execute on your contracts. Every time you take a new project, you are tying up your resources that could otherwise be deployed on another project.

For that reason, it is imperative you carefully select clients and projects. Signing a contract with a bad client is like marrying the wrong person. You are stuck with them for a long time, you'll suffer drama and heartache week to week, and they'll chase your employees away.

Not All Clients Are Good Clients

We intuitively know that not all clients are good clients. Yet often, your worst clients get more attention and faster service than your best clients. Unless you have a strategy in place to intentionally focus on your good clients and fire the bad ones, your employees will get jerked around by demanding, rude, and unappreciative clients. In some cases, they will stop working on a "great" client's project when a "bad" client calls.

When I first started my business, I would take any client that came along. I was focused on growing my small business, and in those early years, new clients were hard to come by. Inevitably I got some bad clients, and I would let them get to me. These clients were overly demanding, unappreciative, sometimes rude, and despite how hard I worked or the great results I achieved, they would try and find a way to lower my fees or not pay at all.

I would agonize about how to repair the relationship, even though I was miserable and losing money working with these clients. There were many nights of lost sleep in the early days, trying to figure out how to keep working with clients that didn't share my values or value my work.

At some point in my development as a business leader, I came to realize that I can't work with every client that comes along. For my own sanity, and ultimately the success and profitability of my business, I needed to make sure that clients were a good fit for my business. For me, this meant that my staff and I enjoyed working with them.

I discovered that if I had a gut feeling that a prospective client would be a troublemaker, my intuition usually proved true: that person or firm ended up being unpleasant to work with. Anecdotally, many of my own clients have told me the same: that they ignored their intuition when first meeting a client only to later confirm that client was horrible to work with.

Ultimately, I decided that I would never lose another night's sleep over money and would never take another client I didn't feel comfortable with or who demonstrated undesirable qualities. My life got a lot better, and my business grew much faster after discovering this important revelation.

In Chapter 6 we will review some strategies for managing difficult clients and possibly either transforming a poor client into a good client – or firing them. And I will share a strategy to graciously help bad clients fire themselves.

In Chapter 2 we looked at how clients either view your services as an expense or an investment. The faster you can determine a client's values, the sooner you can move forward or cut bait. While I'd like to tell you that you can change a cost-focused client to a results-focused client, you probably can't. The only way to have a true value conversation is with a results-focused client. By asking the right questions up front you can figure out if a client is going to want to hear your value points or just keep trying to lower the cost.

I cannot overstate the importance of finding and engaging the right clients. It is the difference between staying small and growing, between high profits and struggling to make payroll.

At the beginning of the Great Recession, I had several engineering clients that went out of business or had to sell for pennies on the dollar when their projects stopped, and they were left with huge receivables and unmanageable debt.

I had other clients that flourished at this time. They were well positioned in recession-proof markets with strong clients or government entities unaffected by the recession. Some were even able to grow and benefitted from choosing among a surplus of talented unemployed candidates eager for work.

Establishing your ideal client criteria is the key to developing a client selection process that ensures you will work with high profit, value-oriented clients.

Who Is Your Ideal Client?

Most professional services firms think they know who their best clients are. This assessment is usually based on two criteria – revenue and relationship. But many are surprised when they take the time to do deeper analysis of their clients. Analyzing the numbers, and a more detailed set of objective and subjective criteria can uncover issues intentionally ignored for years.

One criterion is that your values and the client's values are in sync. In Chapter 8 we will discuss selling on *values*. Selling on values ensures the clients you decide to work with are in harmony with what is important to you. Defining your ideal client must start with your values and whether they match prospective clients'.

I know exactly who my ideal clients are – progressive A&E firms with leaders who are tired of the status quo, want to grow, and are willing to commit time and money to solve their firm's biggest challenges. Often, they have been missing their profit targets, losing employees and/or clients, or constantly having to compete on price. Many of my ideal clients suffer from a lack of organizational accountability and are looking for support from the outside to get important initiatives completed quickly and successfully. While my typical clients are firms with 50-300 employees, I have been very successful with smaller and larger firms. But I have never been successful with a firm that does not share my values or my progressive business approach.

My ideal client is not cheap, old-school, or convinced they can do everything themselves. My experience has told me I can't add enough value or make a significant impact with these types of clients.

A great example of my ideal client is Hillmann Consulting, whose CEO, Chris Hillmann, hired my firm, Jewell & Associates, in 2008 to help them implement the Deltek Vision system. As a Deltek Premier Partner, we successfully helped them transition from an old, obsolete legacy system. I found them to be committed, enthusiastic, open-minded, and easy to work with. Chris engaged us as a valued partner during the six-month project, treating our team with respect and confidence.

As the years passed and I sold my Deltek practice and founded AEC Business Solutions, we have continued to work together on many projects. Chris and his executive team reach out to me for advice on many different areas of the business. They were the first client to sign up for our pilot program when I launched my Find the Lost Dollars training program in 2015, electing to train all 100 employees at the time. Now they are over 250 employees and still growing, with record profits. Chris knows how to invest in his firm and his people to achieve his goals. He has developed a culture focused on excellence, in both client service and business management. This shows that when you are well matched with your ideal client – the results are spectacular – for both parties.

Every time I have taken a client that did not match my ideal client criteria, or even my ideal project criteria, I regretted it. It has caused problems such as failure to achieve goals because of their lack of commitment and effort, disputed fees, and write- offs. Now I am very clear in my proposals what I expect from clients and what it is going to take for them to achieve their goals.

Clients that don't align with your values suck the life out of your business and take attention away from your best clients. It is not worth the added revenue they bring. In the end, most of them are not profitable.

The key point to notice about my ideal client profile is that most of these attributes are psychographic – indicating how the client *thinks* rather than where they are located, how big they are, or what type of A&E firm they are. This may be the case with your ideal clients as well. Getting to the core of who they are, their values, what they want to accomplish, and their propensity to take advice from others may be the key differentiators between your ideal clients and others you'd rather not engage with.

It may also be very important that your clients understand what you do. If you are in a very technical field, it may be critical that your clients are adept at understanding your proposed services and are able to discern one solution from another. Otherwise, you will spin your wheels trying to get them to understand and accept your fees. My solution to this issue with my own clients is to review every proposal with them in detail. This can be very educational and enables them to better understand your project delivery process and design approach. Another valuable approach is to create a document or video explaining your design process. This is most valuable for architects that are working with clients that have never hired an architect before and don't understand how architecture works.

Another important factor that must be considered is whether you truly can deliver value. Can you deliver the outcomes the client expects within their budget? Later, we will look at all the types of expectations a client may have. Your firm may be better at some than others. Some areas may need to be improved to make a particular client happy.

Certain clients will never be happy no matter what you do. They are not your ideal client, even if they provide most of your revenue. Working with miserable clients is not sustainable. You will eventually lose your best employees and fail to grow.

Establishing the criteria for your ideal client should be a thoughtful process with feedback from many stakeholders including employees, subcontractors, and even ex-employees. The process of determining your ideal client criteria can be eye-opening and will give you a basis for future client selection, and current client elimination.

Visit our Resources page at www.aecbusiness.com/RAISEYourValue/ Resources or scan the QR code below for a sample list of ideal client criteria

Get Your Resources

After going through the process of determining your ideal client criteria, you may realize that some of your clients are not a good fit for your firm. Some clients cause you to lose money; others cause you to lose your employees, or your sanity.

It is important to analyze your current clients against your new set of criteria to determine their fit. In my book, Find the Lost Dollars, I prescribe a process of analyzing all clients and assigning them a letter grade of A, B, C, or D. You can then determine what you want to do to retain A clients, improve B clients, and maintain or reduce work with C clients. D clients should be fired.

This type of client rating is the essence of the first step ("Rate") of the 5-Step RAISE Your Value Formula. Rating your clients and establishing your ideal client criteria are essential to raising your value. We will expound on how to rate your clients in Chapter 10 when we review the five steps in detail.

What Makes a Bad Client?

It is just as important to determine what makes a bad client. Your employees and accounting staff can probably identify most of your bad clients easily, even without a list of formalized criteria. They just know what it feels like to work with unappreciative and overly demanding clients that want everything right away, and don't want to pay for it.

You may even determine that certain *types* of clients are less desirable. For example, if you have repeatedly been stiffed by clients in a certain industry, perhaps it does not make sense to work with those types of clients again.

In 2008 when the construction industry crashed, some of my civil engineering clients were owed millions by land developers, who sometimes have shady financing. At that time, many suddenly went out of business and brought down several civil firms that had been around for over 100 years. Two of my clients were dissolved overnight, and the 200 people they employed suddenly lost their jobs.

Bad clients are usually unprofitable clients. Being able to determine their financial requirements and attitudes towards budgets, extra services, and payment expectations will go a long way towards avoiding further losses down the road.

In Chapter 2, we talked about clients that view your services as an expense rather than an investment. This is a key indicator of a bad client, and one that should be avoided. Asking the right questions will help you understand how they perceive your value, and their expectations about the outcomes of the project.

Firing Bad Clients

The 80/20 rule tells us that 20% of our clients are producing 80% of our results. It also explains that 20% of your clients are producing 80% of your financial losses and problems.

Firing your bad clients is essential to achieving lofty growth and profit goals. If you are unable to advocate for your firm by firing bad clients, you will continue to suffer with lower profits and staff turnover.

In almost every case where one of my clients has fired a bad client, their own employees were ecstatic. If your employees are enduring negative treatment by your clients, you better find out and either change the situation or get rid of the client quickly.

My client QK in Clovis, CA found this out a few years ago. While going through the Find the Lost Dollars program, we analyzed their client profitability. We discovered one of their highest revenue, long-time clients was only breaking even. Moreover, this client was a major pain to work with and did not appreciate their staff. With this insight, they decided to raise their rates with the assumption their client would not accept the rate increases. As expected, the client fired themselves and their employees were ecstatic.

But years later, this story took a strange and encouraging twist. Amber Aguayo, CFO and COO of QK, recently sent me this update. It took a while for this client to come to their senses, but this story has a happy ending:

> *"Oddly enough, we are working with them again, with new rates and new client reps from their side and things are going well now. Sometimes you just stand up and hold true and things can turn around.*
>
> *The ironic thing is, our staff requested we work with them again and Janel (former CFO) and I had to be convinced. The problem had been a people issue with an abusive client representative along with a lack of understanding from our staff on fee agreement which was resulting in the client receiving a double discount.*
>
> *Our new fees are now in place with no discount and new*

management by the client. Our current team understands what went wrong last time and is managing expectations in a way that adds real value to the client without compromising on our principles.

Our office management presented a team consisting of a planner, engineer, and a surveyor to align with their existing City team who are both short on staff and experience. This team approach was specifically assembled to support and help them accomplish their objectives.

Our solution wasn't based on price, rather the value created by the service. They are receiving the professional service they need, and we are being fairly compensated with terms and a schedule that allow us to meet our strategic objectives. Our staff are realizing this is how our business can and should operate and, more importantly, is repeatable, consistent, and much less stressful to all."

This story shows that firing a client can actually turn things around. Some clients just have bad people, and those people can go away. Others realize your true value once they start working with another firm that is inferior to yours.

By the way, this same advice goes for bad employees. Another negative result of keeping bad clients is that you are sometimes forced to keep bad employees to handle the higher volume of work. I consistently see firms hiring or keeping mediocre employees to work on unprofitable projects for undesirable clients. This is not a smart business practice.

Bad clients suck the life out of your business. Life is too short – don't continue to suffer with clients or employees that don't meet your standards.

What Do Your Ideal Clients Need and Want?

At a minimum, all clients expect you to deliver on your promises and provide the outcomes you have delineated in your proposal. While quality is difficult to measure and can mean different things to different people, poor quality is usually easy to detect.

Ganesh Kadam, CEO of PMCM Consulting Services in Las Vegas, NV has the following observation about how most clients are willing to pay for quality:

> *"Clients really value the quality of the product. If we provide them quality products, then we keep getting repeat business from them. I have noticed some companies do not include any budget for quality control in their proposals and they miss out on providing quality products. Most [good] clients are fine paying extra for the quality control hours to ensure quality products."*

But beyond the minimum expectations, many firms are not offering all the services their clients need. In most cases, they do not know it. Your clients are hiring other consultants to help them with issues your firm can solve. They do not think to tell you this because you do not ask, and they do not realize the breadth of your team's capabilities.

In some cases, other groups in your firm provide services that your clients want, but they don't know you offer. I have found that unless there is intentional effort to educate employees and clients about all the different services the firm offers, many opportunities to cross-sell are unknowingly lost.

One way to expand your services is to offer additional related services to the projects you are already doing. In some cases, you may have staff that have the needed skills sets or must develop them. In other cases, you may need to partner with another firm or bring in resources to build a new offering.

For example, one of my clients, Capital Engineering, a 65+ person MEP firm headquartered in Sacramento, CA, has a commissioning department offering traditional commissioning, energy efficiency audits, and assessments to building owners. However, they realized that many of their general and sub- contractor clients needed help to manage their own commissioning efforts, so they created a service to help these clients to be the contractor's commissioning manager on projects. This was a clever and creative way to utilize a core strength and get new clients for their engineering design services.

There are many ways to add value to your existing clients without having to go out and hunt for new clients. Your existing clients, especially the ones that already value your work, will be thrilled to hand over work to your firm.

The challenge to learning more about what clients need and want is that some consultants do not listen well. They talk and give advice without really listening to what their client cares about or is expecting. Others are "too busy" to talk with clients except for project related conversations. That is not where you will learn about other opportunities.

Robert Brewer, CPA, CCIFP, Partner and A&E Practice leader at Grassi, CPAs in New York, NY sees this problem in many professional services industries and gives this sage advice:

> *"In every interaction with clients, make sure your staff are doing just as much listening as speaking. As advisors, service providers put so much focus on delivery of advice, results and upsell opportunities that they often forget to be listening for ways in which their clients' businesses and needs are evolving.*

In many cases, we are the ones who can determine where their true needs lie and what their priorities should be, making it essential to ask the right questions, analyze their responses and recommend the services they need to move forward. Of course, the more immersed you are in your knowledge of their industry and operations, the better prepared you will be to identify these needs and solutions."

Here are some questions you can ask that will help you discover additional client needs:

- What are they hiring other consultants to do for them?
- What other services are needed on an annual basis?
- Are there any services they need that you are not offering?
- What new problems do they have (clue – the pandemic has caused many new problems)?
- Do your clients even know all the services you offer (assume they don't)?
- What is their biggest challenge/goal this year?
- Are there any big events or changes happening in their organization including leadership changes, mergers or acquisitions, or organization restructuring that will impact additional services they will need in the future?
- How has the pandemic affected their goals, organizational structure and project needs?

One of the best things you can do is sit down in person with your client and talk with them. One of my clients embarked on an initiative to sit down with their top 30 clients to educate them on all the things their firm did. They physically met with each client, not related to any specific project work, just to get to know their business better and share more information about their capabilities. They were surprised to find that most of their clients had no idea about all the services they offered. That initiative, which took about three months and 30 onsite meetings, generated better relationships and $1.8 million in new revenues.

Your clients are hiring consultants to help them solve problems. You may not be aware of the biggest problems your clients have. By understanding what is stressing them out and keeping them up at night, you can provide additional value beyond your traditional role.

Building a trusted advisor relationship with a client is key to uncovering their biggest challenges. Later we will explore how you can become more of a trusted advisor to your ideal clients.

Client Feedback

It is critical to ask your clients for feedback on a regular basis to understand how you are doing. Are you meeting all their needs? Are they unhappy with any aspects of your services? What could you be doing better? A big part of the client rating we do in the first step of the 5-Step RAISE Your Value formula is evaluating client feedback.

Getting feedback can provide objective data about whether you are delivering the value you have promised. It can also help you understand if there are problematic communication or service issues, and help you correct critical areas clients are not satisfied with.

Sending client surveys is one way to do this. Client Savvy (https://clientsavvy.com/) offers a regular electronic client survey service that probes into key areas such as project performance, client experience, and client service. Ryan Suydam, Chief Experience Officer at Client Savvy, sums up the value of client feedback:

"Asking for feedback regularly – especially during projects – helps you understand how well you are creating value for clients. Are you meeting all their needs? Have you introduced any friction or challenges into their project(s)? Do they have any ideas for ways you can be even more valuable to them?

Gathering client feedback provides objective data about how well you've aligned your value proposition to client expectations. Client feedback helps your internal team align on client service and improving communication internally and externally. Especially when gathered during the project, feedback improves project management, helps mitigate uncompensated scope creep, and assures clients are satisfied before the invoices go out. Happy clients pay their bills faster, and with fewer markdowns.

Firms who regularly collect and act on client feedback are twice as likely to be recommended by their clients, three times more likely to deliver top- quartile business results, and seven times less likely to lose a key client."

Client Experience (CX)

The evolution of CX as a marketing and growth strategy has accelerated in the last ten years. Unfortunately, there are still many professional services firms that are not including CX in their strategic planning or execution. CX accounts for all aspects of what it is like to be a client of your firm, from first touch, through project closeout, and beyond.

According to Ryan Suydam of Client Savvy:

"Research conducted by SMPS in 2019 reveals that Client Experience (CX) is the fastest growing business trend in AEC, with the majority (54%) of marketing leaders reporting

plans to adopt a feedback and/or CX strategy by 2022. Given how easily firms can turn client feedback into sales, profits, and employee retention, this should be on every leader's radar today."

Michael V. Geary, CAE, CEO of Society for Marketing Professional Services (www.SMPS.org) and the SMPS Foundation advises that professional services firms should take a lesson from the Business to Consumer (B2C) industries that have been implementing formal CX programs for years:

"For several years, the Society for Marketing Professional Services (SMPS) and the SMPS Foundation has been reinforcing the need for Business to Business (B2B) firms to transform themselves by, in part, incorporating B2C marketing and customer experience CX strategies.

For example, B2C uses theories of neuroscience to influence how customers make decisions on purchasing services and choosing providers. Corporations have integrated CX programs to capture and retain customers, including tools to measure and respond to client feedback (less than 20% of A/E/C firms have a formal program). Combined, these activities can help firms build customer loyalty, create more value, and ultimately increase revenues."

Clearly there are benefits to implementing a CX program, and with such a low percentage of A&E firms having one, there is enormous opportunity for differentiation and creativity in designing your ideal client experience. Client experience alone can become a key to designing your Winning Advantage, and a reason clients will seek you out and pay you more.

Having a well-developed and reliable client experience process can pay for itself many times over. According to a 2019 *Forbes* article citing 50 customer service related statistics, <u>84% of companies</u> that work to improve their customer experience report an increase in their revenue (Source: <u>https://www.forbes.com/sites/blakemorgan/2019/09/24/50-stats-that-prove-the-value-of-customer-xperience/?sh=1ef708524ef2</u>).

Client experience is much more than just doing what you say you will do, although that is a minimum critical requirement. CX can mean different things to different clients so getting to know your clients and find out how they define the experience they want is an important first step in designing a CX program.

Some of the areas to consider when developing your CX program include:

Onboarding

The client's experience with your staff in the first few days and weeks can make or break your relationship. Having a well-thought-out, documented process for onboarding new clients is an essential first step to high client satisfaction. If you can deliver a "wow" factor that your client will never forget will also help to solidify their opinions of what your firm is like to work with.

Communication

Your CX program should include the how, who, when, what, where and why of communicating with clients. Some clients want more and some less. Do they expect regular status updates? Do your employees email or pick up the phone? Is regular communication something you can build into your scope and charge for?

Relationships

Some clients want deeper relationships with multiple employees in your firm while others are satisfied with working with one key individual. It is important to know what your clients prefer and expect. Also consider the number of people at the clients' organization that you need to build relationships with.

Billing and Financial Practices

Your financial relationship can also matter. Is your billing clear and detailed enough? Does your client feel comfortable with what you are charging them? Having confidence in your financial systems and knowing that your timesheets and invoices are always accurate will go a long way to building trust with clients.

Legal

How does your client feel about the way you negotiate your terms and conditions, legal language, and risk management practices? Some clients will be turned off by an onerous process while others may expect you to have sophisticated risk management policies. This can go both ways as well.

Project Delivery

Do you have a stellar and consistent project delivery process that your client can count on to ensure promised results? Is it clear and consistently applied across your firm, offices, project managers, and leaders? Inconsistent practices can lead to inconsistent results, poor quality and rework, missed deadlines, and increased construction costs, and will turn clients off.

Turnover

There is nothing that will cause you to lose clients faster than turnover. It causes chaos and problems that take away from your firm's success and profits. Sometimes there is nothing you can do about it but having a process in place to communicate and deal with the transition of projects can help.

Too Many Change Orders

Some A&E firms underbid projects and then ask for multiple change orders to make up for low margins. Most clients see right through this strategy and don't like this. If you have implemented the principles put forth in this book so far, you will have aligned expectations with clients and transparent business practices around your fees and their budget. If you are resorting to this type of strategy, you probably don't have the right clients or strategy to begin with.

Premium Services

You may want to consider offering different service levels for different clients. Many firms have different levels of service but don't distinguish them or charge differently for more demanding clients that want a higher level of service.

One way to charge more for premium services is with premium pricing for those clients and offer them both your standard service and premium service at different prices. We will address some ways to do this in Chapter 9 where we look at pricing strategies.

Why Do Your Ideal Clients Select You?

Your ideal clients decide to work with you, hopefully multiple times, because you fulfill their needs and expectations. Are you aware of what needs and expectations you are meeting? Are there any areas that you are not able to satisfy, or they are disappointed in?

It is important to understand why your clients hire you and give you repeat business. Without this knowledge, it is easier to lose them.

Clients will let you go without providing feedback or conveying their disappointment. Suddenly one day you realize they are not giving you more projects. By then it is too late to do anything about it. If you have ever lost a client this way, you know how bad it hurts. Especially if you realize it could have been prevented.

If you know why clients choose to work with your firm, you can ensure higher quality service, and are better able to meet their needs. It is risky to assume you know what they want or why they do business with you.

Some client relationships are only with individual employees. If those employees leave your firm or get reassigned, you can lose clients quickly and silently.

The other benefit to understanding why your clients select you is that you can better develop offers, pricing, and services to new clients. You can also count on references which will more easily help you secure new client commitments.

Visit our Resources page at
www.aecbusiness.com/RAISEYourValue/Resources or scan the QR code below to download a worksheet to reveal why clients select your firm

Get Your Resources

It's Not What You Do, It's What You Deliver

Many firms mistakenly believe they are selected because of their expertise, experience, and qualifications. While these are crucial factors, they are often minimally expected requirements.

If you are focused on selling on your qualifications, you will sound like everyone else. If you want to sound different, and truly sell on value, you must talk about the *outcomes* the client needs, wants, and expects. Clients are not always good at articulating what they want. Without a process to extract from them what they consider are the most important factors for success, you may provide a solution and a price that are out of line with what is needed to win and satisfy the client.

For example, would it be better to say, "We have designed over 50 schools and received three awards for school design" or "Because we have designed over 50 schools, we have a streamlined process to design a more functional, less costly, and easier to maintain school in less time and significantly reduce problems with construction"? Too many firms forget to add the second part of the message which is what the client really cares about. If your ideal client wants a faster, better experience with fewer problems, your firm will stand out from your competitors who are only touting their awards and experience. And because you have your own process, they can't get that process anywhere else. It is even better when the process has a memorable name and acronym, your Proprietary Process, that they can relate to. I'll guide you through creating your own Proprietary Process later in this book.

It's ABOUT Them, Not You

Many firms go on and on about their history, expertise and experience on the ABOUT US page of their web site. But do clients really care about this? Is that why they are looking at your site? It might be more relevant for recruiting purposes, to give a sense of who you are. But for clients, they only care about what you are going to do for them.

Instead, use the ABOUT US space on your web site to talk about the unique outcomes you deliver. It is a perfect place to convey the long-term value of working with and for your firm because of your Unique Value Proposition (UVP) and Proprietary Process. This will truly differentiate your firm from the rest and engage your clients at a different level. In fact, I recommend changing the name of this page from ABOUT US to OUR RESULTS. A separate page specifically for recruiting might be a better way to target ideal employees.

There are many things that consultants do that annoy clients and motivate them to start searching for another firm to work with. Kathleen M. Sharman, CPA, Chief Financial Officer of Greater Orlando Aviation Authority, advises consultants to be better listeners than talkers:

> *"I am looking for a consultant that provides the best value. At a minimum, they must have the right skill set and ability to deliver a quality product that is accurate and delivered within the deadline. Integrity is critical – they must consistently do what they say they will do.*
>
> *But the most important aspect of a stellar client and consultant relationship is when they invest the time to get to know what I want. Nothing aggravates me more than a consultant telling me what I want before they take the time to understand the situation or listen to me explain my vision for the project."*

The Go/No-Go Process

Most firms claim to have a Go/No- Go process – a prescribed method for deciding whether to pursue a project or not. The purpose of the

Go/No-Go process is to keep your firm from wasting money on projects you cannot or should not win. While most firms have some form of a proposal selection process, many ignore low No-Go scores and move forward with proposals for bad projects or clients anyway. In some cases, tens or hundreds of thousands of dollars are lost pursuing projects the firm couldn't or shouldn't win.

The Go/No-Go process is a critical step in deciding whether to pursue a project opportunity. The value of this process is to save the company money by limiting bad choices and increasing the firm's overall win rate. And it can also save money down the road by eliminating the potential for the firm to lose or win a project for which it is not suited or won't profit.

To put together an effective Go/No-Go process, you need to determine the criteria that will help you assess both the likelihood of winning the project, and how successful your firm can be at executing on it. A good Go/No-Go Process should be objective, fair, and scored. You can assign a point system for each criterion to calculate a final score.

An objective score keeps everyone honest. It takes away the emotions and subjective viewpoints of your team members and forces everyone to view potential projects through a lens of prescribed values, intelligence about the project, and evaluation of the client fit – based on your strategy.

If you take the time to develop a strategic plan that elevates the level of clients you want to pursue, but you continue to take clients that do not align with that strategy, you will not get the results you want. This is what is happening in thousands of A&E firms and a key reason they are not hitting profit targets.

A detailed Go/No-Go strategy will analyze the potential of the opportunity in four areas: client relationship, project criteria (including profit analysis), competitor comparison, and team information. The more homework you do, the more accurate the results of the analysis will be. This may not be a viable process for small projects, and you should be investing the appropriate amount of time evaluating and responding to each opportunity that really makes sense, depending on its relative size and potential profitability.

Another important aspect of the Go/No-Go process is to make sure the company is pursuing the "right" projects. You can compare your win rates to your scores over time and determine the minimum score for projects that are worth pursuing—the dividing line between "go" and "no." In looking at your win rate, as well as the level of success you are experiencing in picking the right projects to bid on and accept, there is an inherent ROI you are realizing from your investment in proposals on which you are bidding. By understanding the cost of each lost proposal and the criteria used to pick the winning team, you can start to define a Go/No-Go strategy and criteria that are more appropriately rewarding your efforts.

Scores from your Go/No-Go process should be tracked along with the win-loss statistics from your opportunities. Comparing the Go/No-Go score against your win-loss rates will give you a better measure over time of your success and how your pursuit decisions correlate with winning.

I recommend capturing the Go/No-Go data in your system, if possible. The figure below shows the scoring section of a sample Go/No-Go used by some of my clients that has been programmed into their Client Relationship Management (CRM) system:

Project Go/Get Calculation		
Project Materialization		
Prob. of Project Authorization (65%)	100	%
Prob. of Project Funding (35%)	80	%
Project Probability Baseline	93.00	%
Our Competitive Success Probability	58	%
☑ Use GoNoGo EvalScore		
Compound Probability	53.94	%
Use Go/Get Weighted Rev in Forecasts ☑		
Go/Get Weighted Revenue	$	2966700.00
Costs		
Est. Revenue from Gen'l. Tab	$	5500000.00
Est. Building Const. Cost		120,000,000.00

Visit our Resources page at
www.aecbusiness.com/RAISEYourValue/Resources or scan the QR
code below to download a sample Go/No-Go Evaluation Form

Get Your Resources

Douglas Reed, P.E, a leading expert in business strategy for engineering and environmental firms, author of Lead a Movement: The Insider's Guide to Powerful Strategy Execution (https://www.fostergrowth.biz/book/), and CEO of Meridian Associates in Beverly, MA recounts how implementing a strict Go/No-Go process for one of his former clients radically improved win results, reduced costs, and improved profits:

> *"A poorly performing environmental firm conducted a three-day sales training program that included the creation of a scoring system to rate potential clients and projects. The new mantra was to restrict pursuits to those who scored high. The main point was to limit overhead hours to where the outcome was likely to support the company's strategic goals.*
>
> *The first challenge was to withdraw from a publicly advertised procurement that had a value of several hundred thousand dollars. The client was trying to dodge environmental laws, hiding behind an engineering firm that would identify excuses. We were the incumbent on an earlier phase. Because of our new criteria to only work with environmentally responsible clients, we withdrew from consideration. Our competitors were surprised. We knew what we were doing.*
>
> *Next, the CEO had a personal desire to work with the state's largest water and wastewater utility. But scoring for that client showed they failed our test. They only selected consultants on price and had demonstrated a litigious bent. When confronted with the facts, the CEO nonetheless decided to write the proposal over the Thanksgiving holiday, off the company clock. He was the boss so what could we do?*

We had the highest prices and did not win the work. The CEO's wife was very unhappy that he spent this vacation working on a proposal. I really didn't need to say more. The CEO fell in line and never did this again. These are valuable lessons to learn.

A third opportunity was with a client that scored high. They loved innovation, the commissioner was very respected in the industry, and we had a great track record with them. We launched a coordinated effort with our teaming partners to strengthen relationships with all decision influencers and learn their key concerns. It took more than a year, but the outcome was a win for the second largest combined sewer overflow project in the state with fee values over $10 million.

It has taken a lot of discipline to turn work away, but it is worth it. Having a strict Go/No-Go process saved us a lot of wasted overhead cost. We focused only on the pursuits that met our criteria. Our proposal costs dropped by 20%, we submitted two- thirds fewer proposals and we won 70% of them. Our backlog doubled and profits hit a company record. All of this started by adopting a sales process that identified that the first decision of working with a client is ours, and to only invest in those we have decided are worthy."

It is incumbent on leadership to have the discipline and resolve to say NO to bad projects and clients. One argument I hear a lot is that good clients will sometimes ask you to do bad projects – projects that have low budgets or are too small to make a profit. While you may be reluctant to say no to your good clients, it should be part of your strategy to increase your fees substantially on these projects to make it worth your while. Refusing a great client is difficult, so don't simply say no. Help them realize how the "bad projects" are costing your firm money and taking a toll on their other projects. Add a premium for projects of a certain type or under a certain size. If they truly are a great client, they will understand and pay extra to have you on the team.

CHAPTER 6

Dealing with Tough Clients

"Your most unhappy customers are your greatest source of learning."

- Bill Gates

L ife would be perfect and business would be a breeze if all clients were patient, understanding, and agreeable. But they're not. They can be demanding, unreasonable, and even hostile to work with. This takes a toll on everyone and can cause employees to feel tremendous stress, or even want to quit.

You must manage the climate your team is exposed to and get rid of damaging clients before they destroy your culture. One way to do this is to ensure you do not get them in the first place. However, once they have slipped by your screening process, you must take action to mitigate the damage they can do, financial, emotional, or otherwise.

It is important to let employees know that your policy is not to work with awful clients, and they need to report any unacceptable behavior to management. Without this clear direction, employees will silently suffer the burden of rude communication or unacceptable behavior from clients until they prematurely leave. Having a process to handle inappropriate language or behavior will empower employees and make them feel safe and valued.

Having a culture based on values of respect, character, and kindness will guide your firm's hiring, client selection and relationships with vendors and business partners. To maintain that culture requires consistency, and possibly training for managers and leaders to be able to deal with conflicts.

One caveat I will add to this discussion is that sometimes the disagreeable client is right. They may have a legitimate complaint that needs our attention. The most important thing we can remember is to have an open mind going into difficult conversations.

Managing Difficult Conversations

One of the hardest things that A&E leaders must do is manage unhappy clients. Problems are naturally going to occur on your projects. While you can prevent some of them – others are out of your control.

And clients do not like surprises. The worst conversations you can have with a client is explaining how a problem, that you could have prevented, is going to cause their project to cost more or take longer.

Clients hire us to help them avoid those types of problems. That is why I have put so much emphasis on prevention, rather than mitigation.

Over the years I have dealt with hundreds of client problems. In my 24 years working with Deltek, I had to skillfully manage high tension situations caused by software problems, hardware problems, support issues, upgrades, financial disputes and other common challenges in the software implementation world (I'm sure some of you can relate).

I learned some valuable lessons and I want to share a few of them below. They illustrate how addressing issues quickly can help keep a problem from getting worse:

Bad News Never Gets Better with Time

Talk with your client as soon as you discover an issue. The longer you wait, the worse it will get. By dealing with a problem quickly, you may prevent the problem from getting much worse. This is an important practice to teach your employees and make a regular point of discussion with examples.

A prime example of this is that PMs often avoid dealing with out-of-scope changes and getting change orders approved. They kick the can, leaving time charges accumulating and hope they will have money "left over" that they can make it up with later. They also avoid conflict, waiting to discuss a problem until it blows up. It does not get easier to ask a client for money later. And no – there will not be money left over to make it up.

Set Expectations Before Starting the Project

The best way to deal with problems is to not have them at all. Skip Weisman, leadership and communication expert for professional services businesses, has the following advice regarding avoiding problems with clients:

> "You can eliminate 80-90% of tough clients and tough client conversations by communicating more thoroughly on the front end of the relationship, and by that, I mean well before the sale is closed and the bid is awarded.
>
> But to have the type of communication that is required to get the client relationship right, so that it leads to a win-win-win outcome (a win for you, a win for the client, and a win for the ultimate end users of the project), you have to be absolutely clear on your business model and the steps you require to get the right type of projects.

It is critical to know your non-negotiable and non-compromising values, what you need and expect from the client so that you can do your best work for them, your specific commitments to the client and what they can expect from you. In my consulting projects I call this section of my agreement "Joint Accountabilities". It provides a great upfront framework against which we can measure each other's performance.

In my experience with A&E clients, most do not put the work in like I'm suggesting. Most just "wing it," leading to stress for all involved and much lower profitable project outcomes for the firm.

Having what you may consider a tough conversation on the front end around joint expectations and accountabilities significantly reduces the need for you to have even tougher conversations after your client is onboard and your project has begun."

Setting expectations must be part of your sales process. Without a plan to avoid common issues, you will continue to have the same problems repeatedly. Later we will discuss how to develop an effective sales process that helps ensure you win AND avoids common, predictable problems.

Watch Out for Yellow Lights

Do not speed through yellow lights! Yellow lights are a sign to *slow down*. They signify potential problems that can develop into more serious issues.

One example that illustrates this point is when your client has turnover on their project team. There is often a significant delay in getting a new person up to speed. If the new person is not as experienced as the previous client reps, this can cause other issues including cost overruns, disputes, and refusal to approve change orders. By expressing concerns early on, and putting preventive solutions into place, problems may be avoided or mitigated.

Another example is when a client won't take your advice or comply with required regulations. I once worked with an environmental consulting firm in the mid-Atlantic that was working on a land development project that included an area of wetlands. Their client was arguing with them about compliance with turtle reclamation requirements imposed by state law. They did not want to spend the time and money to follow the regulations. My client stopped working on the project until the issue was resolved. They had to educate the client about the severe repercussions of ignoring the law until they were finally able to get the client to agree to comply. If they had just moved forward with doing what the client wanted, against their better judgement and values, the consequences could have been costly for both the firm and their client.

I Have a Concern

Do not be afraid to challenge a client that you can see is clearly going down the wrong road or ignoring a glaring problem. They may want to argue with you about it at first, and ultimately may not take your advice. If they do take your advice, you may prevent a serious problem. If they don't, they will remember that you tried to help them avoid the issue.

This is particularly important if a client has unrealistic expectations about how long something should take. Instead of killing your staff to meet an unrealistic deadline, and compromising other projects in the process, be upfront with the client and educate them about why their deadlines are impossible. Often clients just push hard to get what they want but will back down when presented with a good argument.

In my consulting practice, we taught our consultants to say, "I have a concern." Having a specific way to deal with these tough conversations can make it easier for your staff to have them.

Pick Up the Phone

Too many people today use a passive- aggressive method to deal with problems – email. Email does not convey concern at the same level as two people talking on the phone or better, in person. Save yourself potential misunderstanding and build a better relationship with your client at the same time by picking up the phone and calling. If nothing else, they will know your concerns are important if you choose to call instead of emailing.

Negative Feedback Is a Gift

Most people get upset when they receive criticism. I believe negative feedback is a gift. Most clients are not honest enough to tell you how they really feel, and will just go ahead and complain to others, or worse, hire another consultant. Take feedback for what it is – a way to improve. Asking for feedback and proactively resolving their issues also shows your concern and desire to please your client.

Educating Clients

The most important thing you can do for your client is to teach them. Not only will they be able to make better decisions during the project, but you will have a more educated client to work with and will appreciate your effort to improve their understanding and results.

Most of your clients do not really understand what you do. Even if you are an engineer subcontracting to an architect, they rely on you to design the best solution for the client. It is always easier to deal with a client that understands the nuances of how to make the right choices. It also helps them to focus on making the smartest decisions instead of just focusing on cost.

Another benefit to educating clients is terminology. If you work in a technical field, it can be especially frustrating when consultants throw around complex-sounding terms. Don't always assume they know what you are talking about or the meaning of design and construction terminology.

Clients will value you when you slow down and take the time to teach them. The sales process is a perfect time to start educating them as it differentiates you. Most consultants like to show how much they know. They like to dazzle clients with technical-sounding words so the client will be intimidated and rely on them for help. But that strategy often backfires – most clients do not want to be told what to do. They want to make educated decisions after considering all the options.

Keep it Simple

When you confuse clients, it is harder for them to make decisions. In sales, confusion leads to "analysis paralysis". As Nick Kane of Janek Performance Group writes:

> *"As sales professionals, we want to make sure we meet the needs of customers so that we can become trusted advisors. But sometimes, in a rush to be sure we fulfill those needs, we overload the customer with too much information and too many options. The customer is then left dizzy, dazed and confused, and backs away from us, eventually later choosing someone who simplified their options and was not overwhelming."*

> *(Source:https://www.janek.com/blog/how-analysis-paralysis-can-hurt-your- sales-and-productivity/)*

Selling to Public Agencies

Working in the government arena can be challenging. There can be more competition, more regulation, more risk, and limits on rates.

Many firms have taken the philosophy that the only way to make money is with volume.

In working with clients that make their living in government contracting, particularly with state and local agencies, they have resigned themselves to the false belief that they cannot make more than the prescribed profit limit that the government has set. And even worse, by allowing scope creep to erode their profits, they often make much less.

But there are firms out there making 20% plus profits on government work. That is not to say it is easy, but by offering niche services and developing effective relationships, certain government clients can work magic to hire who they want.

With State and Local agencies, there can be more challenges but making a good profit is possible. It is important to understand the laws governing the agencies you work with, as well as their restrictions on executive compensation and overhead expenses. Depending on which area you focus on, the competition can be deeper and the mandate to select on price required. The methods prescribed in this book cannot change that. What we can do is help you to decide if it is worth your time, investment, and future by competing on price.

The 1972 Brooks Act established the procurement process of qualifications-based selection (QBS) by which A&E firms are selected for design contracts with federal design and construction agencies. Unfortunately, some agencies will still choose to select on price, intentionally ignoring the Brooks Act requirements.

If you choose to do work with agencies that select on price, realize that it can be very difficult to make a profit. Unless your scope is reduced or you can use less experienced staff on these projects, you can even lose money with low fee projects. Other firms will make the decision to get away from the commodity trap that some public agencies have established.

We all know this is not fair, and that the taxpayer is not really getting a better deal. Firms that sell on price will cut their quality, pay lower salaries to their staff, take longer to deliver, have more change orders, and other disadvantages from the clients' standpoint. Some clients have learned the hard way. Others are stuck and can't change the rules.

This story from a long-time A&E industry consultant illustrates the trap that government agencies get in when they select on price:

> *"Each year a certain public agency would invite design consultants to the agency headquarters for a design consultants coordination meeting. At one of these meetings, the agency director announced that consultant selection would no longer be accomplished by a qualification-based selection (QBS) process. He stated that a QBS selection process was too time consuming and expensive for agency staff. Instead, design contracts would be awarded to the consultant with the lowest lump sum bid. It was explained that the consultant would be given enough preliminary design information on which the consultant could base its bid for the entire design. The agency represented that any experienced and qualified consultant should know how much a design should cost. The consultants grumbled, but to no avail.*

> *As the design process began, it became apparent that the preliminary design information provided by the agency was inadequate. The consultant's preliminary design efforts revealed that there needed to be changes in the contract scope of services. The consultant's request for an amended scope of services with commensurate additional*

compensation was denied. The agency argued that the request was ineligible since the contract was for a lump sum amount for the entire design. No amount of protest from the consultant community produced any relief. The consultants predictably lost money and sought to find ways to reduce the cost of their designs. This effort was largely unsuccessful as compromising quality to improve their profitability conflicted with their standards of professionalism.

At the following year's design consultants coordination meeting, the director stated that the agency had been receiving poor quality designs resulting in schedule delays while corrections to designs were being made. He went on to say that when projects were advertised for construction bids, constructability problems were found by the contractors. This resulted in bid date delays while corrections to the design were being made. During construction, a higher-than-normal number of expensive change order claims by contractors were common. The Director stated that the agency had heard the consultants, accepted that going to a bidding selection process had not been successful, and was returning to a QBS process for selecting consultants.

The agency's ill-conceived effort to commoditize the selection of engineering design services was a failure. It had been a costly embarrassment for the agency and the consultants had experienced significant financial losses plus an increased risk of professional liability claims. "

While government contracting can be challenging, there are positive aspects of pursuing government work, despite conditions that can make it impossible to realize profits over 10%.

When you can secure a lump sum contract, you have more control over your profit margin. By accurately estimating the scope of work and level of effort to deliver the clients' requirements and ensuring a desirable profit margin and contingency fee are included, a well-managed project can be highly profitable.

I have helped clients realize 20% to 30% profits on government jobs by closely monitoring costs and working diligently to prevent overruns. Having tight project management and a defined project delivery and quality control process is critical to achieving high profits on any project, let alone government projects.

With any kind of client, residential, institutional, commercial, or public, there can be good and bad clients. When you develop your criteria for your ideal client, you may need different sets of criteria depending on the type of client you are pursuing.

I am not saying you should not take public work. The world depends on architects and engineers to improve the way we live, help us get around safely, and provide government services and schools for our children. But I am suggesting that your strategy should enable you to get the highest profits possible, and with the strategies, methods, and tools provided in this book, you can balance this work with higher fee work and still achieve top-level profits.

Challenges of Subcontracting

Many of you reading this book are subcontractors to prime contractors, architects, or other companies that have primary contracts with clients financing your projects. As a sub, you may experience a lack of control, unfavorable terms and conditions, lack of access to the end client, and failure to get reimbursed from scope creep.

Unless the client you are subcontracting to has your back, you can lose significant profits from poor management and failure to stick up for your positions when issues arise. This is a key factor in deciding who to work for.

But subs are not always treated well. Clients do not always help you get change orders and are often afraid to go to bat for you with clients. They may have bad accounting and management practices themselves which can negatively impact your firm. These are all factors when deciding if working as a sub for these clients makes sense.

As with all the other advice in this book, who you choose to work with as a sub can make or break your success. When you decide to give up control, it is critical to only subcontract to clients you can trust.

Once you are in a subcontracting relationship, it becomes even more important to stick to your guns in negotiating fees and change orders, and ensure you have favorable terms that enable you to get reimbursed when conditions change.

Having an extremely well-defined and detailed scope of services and tight proposal and contract language will help protect you in the event your client tries to get you to do work outside of the scope for free, or if they are not paying you as promised.

I have seen plenty of clients that use their subcontractors to finance their businesses. They put in place pay-when-paid contract terms and then do not pay you timely when the client pays them. This float enables them to manage their cash at your expense.

When I first started my career in the A&E industry, I was a 20-something software consultant selling and implementing the Wind2 software to architecture and engineering firms. One of my clients in Washington, DC was a 30-person architecture firm mostly working with the State Department and General Services Administration (GSA).

I worked closely with the managing principal of the firm, helping him with bookkeeping including billing, accounts payable, accounts receivable, payroll and financial reporting. Every month when I was cutting checks to pay the subs and vendors, he would divvy up the money, often not paying subs he owed money to. This was the early 1900s and times were lean. This firm financed their cash flow on the backs of their engineers by having pay-when-paid payment terms, and then taking their time to pay them even after their client had paid them.

Inevitably, I would be sitting at his desk (these were the days when software was on one computer in the office), and an engineer would call asking for payment. Tom, my client would take the call. Then he would get off the phone, and say, "Dammit, cut them a check."

I learned early in my career that the squeaky wheel gets the oil. These subs would never have been paid if they had not called. They learned quickly that they had to stay on top of this client to get paid.

I would say this is still the norm in the A&E industry, even 30+ years later, but there is no reason to put up with this kind of treatment. It was hard to get work back then, which deterred subcontractors from sticking up for themselves. With work so plentiful and demand for A&E services so strong, now is the time to raise prices and refuse to be treated badly by clients.

CHAPTER 7

Uncover Your Hidden Value & Design Your Winning Advantage

"Price is what you pay. Value is what you get."

- Warren Buffet

Now you know how important it is to identify your ideal client and figure out what they want. For you to design a Winning Advantage, you must uncover the value you bring to your clients. Unfortunately, many firms do not identify, articulate, or even realize their value. Their value has been hidden and not leveraged to get better clients or increase prices.

When you can clearly demonstrate your unique value, your ideal clients will stop trying to reduce your fees. They will want to work with you because the value you provide is far greater than the fees you charge. This is called your Winning Advantage. Your Winning Advantage is made up of two elements: your Unique Value Proposition (UVP) and Proprietary Process.

To determine where you add value, you must dive deep into your projects. What makes your firm successful? How do you affect outcomes? Where do you save clients' money in unexpected ways? Why do clients praise you? What differentiates your firm from other consultants they have hired? Your staff are often the key to understanding where you add value.

To get to the root of your value, you must analyze many successful projects and determine the quantitative and qualitative qualities that produced successful results. Do not be afraid to quantify (attach a dollar figure to) long term expected cost savings, immediate expenses you saved your client, or unexpected problems that were diffused or avoided.

The key to designing your Winning Advantage is figuring out which of the five key differentiators to leverage.

Five Ways to Differentiate

There are five ways to differentiate your services and firm from your competitors. Your UVP and proprietary process must include at least one but ideally several of the following five qualities:

1. **Price**

    Price is the easiest differentiator. You can differentiate by being the least expensive or the most expensive provider. If you are somewhere in between, you are not differentiated and must rely on the remaining four differentiators to convince clients to select you over less expensive options.

    Pricing is a very important strategic decision. If you decide to be the low-cost provider, you must find a way to cut costs and still offer a decent service. Low cost prohibits you from offering high quality in a fast way (remember Good/Fast/Cheap – you can only have two).

    If you decide to be the highest priced service provider in your market, you will need to have many other differentiators that drive perceived high value. Your client must value the qualities that make you more desirable and believe that the value they will get is greater than the "expensive" price.

It is also possible to differentiate on price because of the unique way you offer your services. In Chapter 9 we will explore some strategic pricing methods that enable you to appear different than everyone else.

2. **Brand**

   Your brand is your perceived reputation in your industry. If you have brand differentiation, you must deliver on the brand 100 percent of the time. Even a few "bad reviews" or problem projects can erode your brand.

   Our earlier discussion about values is critical to the formation of your brand. Your values drive your brand. The two must always be in alignment.

   From your clients' viewpoint, your brand is the recognition and expectation of what they will be getting from working with you. Firms that are effective at building a distinguished brand can charge higher prices. Some clients will seek you out – and pay more – just to have the opportunity to work with you. Certainly, this happened with world famous architects like Frank Lloyd Wright and Frank Gehry. They were able to name their price because of the status of working with them.

   You can also have brand recognition in a very specific niche market. It could be a specific type of project, limited geography, type of client, or all three.

   A good example of this is HOK, a firm known for designing innovative and sustainable sports stadiums. If you Google "best architect for NFL stadiums," they show up multiple times organically on the first page. What is your firm known for? Do you have a niche market or is there a phrase that you own in search engines where your firm always comes up?

Building a world class brand is an intentional effort. Your marketing messages, clientele and quality of your work must be on point. If you dabble with high-end clients and also take low-end cheap clients, you will damage your brand and lose your differentiated status.

3. **Technology**

   There are many ways that technology can be used to differentiate. Here are a few:

   a. You can be more efficient with your services
   b. Automation can enable you to deliver more consistent results
   c. You can offer more innovative solutions that no one else has
   d. Your marketing methods can be more effective and consistent
   e. Your brand and thought leadership can be built around high-tech topics
   f. You can attract different types of employees with a tech-driven culture
   g. You can utilize technology on your projects that no one else has, or use it differently
   h. You can offer different products and services than your competitors

Michael Davis is the Chief Strategy Officer at WGI, a 600+ associate consulting engineering, planning, environmental, and geospatial firm based in West Palm Beach, Florida. He describes how they are using technology as a competitive advantage:

> *"We have built WGI around strong project management with technology and innovation-driven project delivery*

practices. In 2021 we purchased a software company that builds water models and applications for forecasting flooding. We are a very strategic planning-centric firm with a history of successful growth both organically and through acquisitions with technology as a core competitive advantage."

Technology is a great way to differentiate, however it isn't always easy. Over the years I have seen many A&E firms develop software and other tools for specific projects and then never use them again. Many engineering firms in particular struggle to leverage new technology to be competitive.

4. **Service/Team** -

Differentiating on service is difficult because everyone claims to provide great services. Go to any of your competitors' web site and see what they say about their service. Everyone uses the same adjectives: reliable, innovative, client-focused, etc.

When you can show how your service produces results your ideal client wants – then you actually appear different. This can be demonstrated by designing a unique client experience and providing proof how it will ensure their success. It is critical to be able to communicate this difference in a persuasive way that truly shows your higher-level service and successful outcomes.

Many firms struggle with consistency in the way they deliver and manage projects, communicate, and charge for their work. If you can create your unique Proprietary Process around client service, or a combination of service and process, you will truly differentiate your firm from others in the industry.

ENR 500 top ten firm Gannett Fleming differentiates on service by how they invest in their employees. Paul Nowicki, President and COO says this about this focus:

"The AEC business is rapidly commoditizing, through consolidation, outsourcing and technology advancement. Our market position and growth are dependent on our ability to invest into our people to become thought leaders and innovators. This is our differentiator and value proposition to our clients. "

Clearly, this strategy is using several of the five differentiators - service/team, brand and technology - to position Gannett Fleming in their markets.

In rare cases, you can differentiate if your team has extremely rare experience your clients can't get anywhere else. In this case, if your client needs your service to get their project completed, you can almost charge what you want.

5. Process

If you can do things in a way that no one else can and show how that process delivers results your ideal client values, then it is difficult to compare your firm to your competitors. Having a Proprietary Process is one of the greatest ways to gain a Winning Advantage.

Below I will show you how to develop your own Proprietary Process that you can use to design a Winning Advantage to differentiate your firm and services.

Your Unique Value Proposition (UVP)

Your UVP is your firm's silver bullet for getting better clients and higher fees. It takes unique value that you uncover in Step 3 of the 5-Step RAISE Your Value Formula and turns it into a clearly defined set of benefits that no one else can deliver. It is your firm's unique elevator speech focused on the exact way you add value to your ideal clients. It differentiates your services so they can't be commoditized.

For example, my UVP is front and center on the home page of my web site. It is my brand promise that attracts my ideal clients to want to work with me.

> ## WE HELP A&E FIRMS MASTER BUSINESS AND PROJECT MANAGEMENT
>
> *Our Find the Lost Dollars online business training for A&E Firms is guaranteed to increase your utilization rate, cash flow and project profits.*

For my ideal clients in search of higher profits, the fact that I *guarantee* my services takes away the risk of investing in training their employees. The other key to this UVP is that I am very specific about the outcomes they will get ("increase your utilization rate, cash flow, and project profits.")

What can you confidently promise your clients? How can you reduce their risk, help them get a bigger return on investment on their projects, or help them avoid serious issues in the design and construction process? One way you can provide proof of success is to specify how many projects you have successfully completed on budget and schedule. Of course, this requires that you have done this!

The best way to develop your UVP is to start with your projects and employees. Brainstorming in groups and dissecting successful project outcomes will help you uncover your hidden value. Step 3 of the 5-Step RAISE Your Value Formula – Investigate – will take you step by step through the process of uncovering your unique value and developing your UVP which your staff can learn to communicate more effectively with ideal clients.

Training Employees to Deliver the Message

Even if the leaders of your firm have a strong command of your value, many of your employees do not. In fact, if you asked ten employees the simple question, "Who are we and what do we do?" you would probably get ten radically different answers, not focused on client results.

The value message is useless if everyone can't deliver it. Value must come from everyone in your firm in all conversations and interactions with clients. When implementing the RAISE Your Value formula, training your staff is a key component to success.

Before your employees can even learn to recite your value proposition messages, they need to gain an understanding of key business management principles so they can truly comprehend the concept of value versus price from the clients' standpoint.

In our Find the Lost Dollars business management training program, we work with firms in groups of ten to 20 project managers and leaders to incorporate business acumen and financial management skills into daily behaviors. In just twelve weeks we see PMs with no business focus transform into future leaders who know what to do to control project costs and help their firm succeed. This gives them confidence to have money conversations with clients.

Lisa Wallis-Dutra, Senior Engineer at QK based in Clovis, California went through the Find the Lost Dollars training and explains how it helped her see the value she is bringing to clients:

> *"While I have always been concerned for the client, the company, project performance and profits, as an engineer my focus has always been on the technical aspect of the work. This focus on quality and technical excellence will never change. What has changed, however, is my behavior and focus on how the technical discipline and the project management disciplines are inextricably tied. By changing the way I look at and value project management, I am helping my company serve our clients better AND Find Lost Dollars!*

I am helping my clients and our company in a number of ways including setting specific scopes, forecasting what our process to alter the course will be "when" something changes, preparing a painless mechanism to handle adjustments to projects, and reviewing scopes, schedules, and fees with the client up front and at each stage of the project. I used to be uncomfortable asking for amendments or funding increases. This course helped me realize that this reality is a regular part of meeting project objectives for the client. Because I have taken the time to be clear throughout the process, these conversations are just that—continuing conversations of the project without concern or that dreaded feeling that I am asking for money.

This realization that the project management is not an add-on, or instead of my technical expertise, has allowed me to value the time I am spending answering difficult questions for my clients, or otherwise dealing with the administrative duties that are necessary to meet the project objectives. I am treating this management and my discussion with the clients as a service and have realized that it is billable— because it is a value-added service and one that the client needs and appreciates. Again, because I am in the habit of quantifying scopes, I have taken the same approach with my results."

Business-focused training was able to help Lisa and many other PMs at their firm feel more comfortable talking with clients about money and the value of sound project management practices. Don't assume all your managers understand the real value of project management. This is where a lot of lost dollars leak from projects. Often, PM time is disregarded and not charged to clients, believing they won't pay for it. **If your clients don't value project management, how can they value your PMs?**

Once managers and leaders have embraced the importance of the firm's business practices, such as asking for change orders, monitoring project costs, or attending client meetings, it can be easier to work with your team to consistently convey the value message. Many firms have not addressed this gap in PM understanding and are missing out on a huge opportunity.

Scott Butcher, FSMPS, CPSM, Director, Strategic Growth Advisory at Stambaugh Ness, relates the importance of managers being trained to deliver an effective value message:

> *"This industry is rife with exceptional doers who get promoted into management positions even though they haven't been properly trained to be managers. They often can't even deliver effective value messages, which is important for every single employee within a company – top to bottom.*
>
> *They need to ask themselves, 'Why would someone hire my firm or my practice? What makes us different than the competition? What is the client truly trying to accomplish?' In other words, what does the client or prospect really care about, because it's not that you have a professional license, deliver projects or time or on budget, or have been involved with ten similar projects. That's about you. A value message must be about the client. Only then will you be able to successfully communicate meaningful, impactful reasons for them to work with your firm. Everything else is just mundane and unoriginal."*

Your Unique Proprietary Process

The second tool you will create in the RAISE Your Value Formula is a Proprietary Process. Combined with your UVP, you will have an unbeatable Winning Advantage.

Your Proprietary Process is an acronym of an exciting word that means something to your firm—just like the word RAISE is itself an acronym. Each letter signifies a strong value benefit that appeals to your ideal client or describes a process your firm utilizes that no one else has.

This will differentiate you because many firms struggle to be consistent in everything they do – from quality control to managing extra services to client service – and this lack of consistency causes great problems for clients and employees. Without a consistent process, your staff will underperform and there will be more surprises in every project. Adhering to a unique Proprietary Process helps ensure consistency and makes it easier to talk about what you do. If it ties into your values, even better.

The acronym describing this process should simply explain what you do, how it is different, and why it gets results. The best way to communicate your unique process is to give it a catchy name and a graphic image that illustrates the process.

For your process to be unique, you must identify parts of your process that are unique. These unique aspects to your process should directly relate to how you solve common problems your clients have. When you can show how your unique process has worked for other clients, you will stand out from your competitors. For example, my firm, AEC Business Solutions (https://aecbusiness.com/), has the Find the Lost Dollars process, a 3-step process that we graphically explain on our web site and in our digital marketing materials.

When someone asks what I do, I tell them, "We have a proven 3-step process to transform technical professionals into business leaders, improve business practices in A&E firms, and increase profits 3% to 5% per year." Then I simply describe the three steps whose corresponding acronym forms my company name:

AEC = Assess + Educate + Create – which is graphically depicted below, simplifies a complex concept so that prospective clients can easily understand what we do. It uses language that is clear about the end results and benefits our clients will get when they work with us.

A = Assess

We utilize a business management assessment survey that delves into the strengths and weaknesses of your firm and scores nine areas of the business by people, processes and systems. This assessment helps us uncover where lost dollars can be found and gives your employees the ability to provide feedback and suggestions for improvement. No one else has this type of assessment and can provide this benefit to A&E firms.

E = Educate

We have the only online business management training program for A&E leaders, PMs and their staff guaranteed to increase profits in a few months.

C = Create

We help A&E firms create new processes, improve systems and implement business best practices that increase efficiency, reduce costs, and increase revenue and profit.

Having a unique way to talk about our program and keeping it simple and free of tech language is appealing to our ideal clients.

Another example of an effective Proprietary Process is Scott Oldford's ROI method. Scott is a marketing consultant who helps small online businesses scale using his unique, three- step methodology. ROI stands for Relevancy, Omnipresence, and Intimacy. It is a clever way to concisely explain what he does and differentiate himself from all other thought leaders in his field.

The most important part of your Proprietary Process is that you can actually deliver the results that you tout. If you claim to have a Quality Assurance/Quality Control (QA/QC) process but your quality is not consistent, your Proprietary Process will appear to be misleading or false.

In Chapter 10 we will look at how to make the Proprietary Process part of your marketing, project delivery, client communication and business management practices. Execution is the key to leveraging your Proprietary Process and ensuring client satisfaction and results.

Your Proprietary Process should clearly show how you add value and reduce risk throughout your project lifecycle. From project initiation to project closeout there should be an established, documented process for how you treat clients, manage the work, produce deliverables and run the business. You must also ensure there is corresponding training, so employees are well-versed on how to run projects and deal with clients. Helping our clients develop and document processes is one of my firm's sweet spots, and we can help you do this if you need help.

Clients Will Pay for Certainty

One of my key mantras in life is that **no one likes surprises** (except for surprise parties and marriage proposals). What will upset a client more than almost anything are "surprises" that delay their project or fail to give them the results they were expecting. Paying more for a consultant that reduces risk, removes obstacles, and eliminates potential problems is like buying an insurance policy.

I don't believe most of the problems that occur on your projects should be surprising. If you have executed more than a few similar projects, you can easily put together a list of things that can go wrong. Figuring out how to avoid or plan for them and educating your client in advance to eliminate surprises will massively differentiate your firm from your competitors. If this can become part of your Proprietary Process, your clients will be extremely impressed, value your service, and pay you generously for it.

For example, a few years ago I worked with a client during a major Deltek system implementation. I was hired by the client to help manage the implementation, even though they already had a Deltek partner assisting them. They viewed me as an insurance policy to reduce problems and keep the project on course. I interviewed their staff to determine what issues might occur so that I could prepare the client for potential problems. After interviewing one employee pivotal to the implementation success, I predicted that she was likely to quit within weeks. Even though she had worked at the engineering firm for 20 years, it was obvious to me that she was not interested in going through the complex process of learning a new system. I was able to give my client a heads up and get the ball rolling on hiring a replacement while accounting for her likely departure in our implementation plan. As I predicted, she left within a few weeks despite her claims to the contrary. My client really appreciated my insight and was relieved that we had been able to get a jump on recruiting a new person.

In Chapter 10 we will explore some methods for building a library of solutions to common problems your clients face.

Commodity Versus Trusted Advisor

Andrea P. Howe, co-author of *The Trusted Advisor Fieldbook,* writes,

> *"You will not become a trusted advisor through great marketing programs, great presentations, or even great blogs or tweets. Trust is created in your exchanges with others—especially one-on-one."*

As we can see in the figure below, there are five distinct types of client relationships. The most impactful of these is the trusted advisor, the perch atop the pyramid where few consultants are able to ascend. To become a trusted advisor requires intentional focus on building trust and developing a strong bond with your clients. When you are a trusted advisor, clients are no longer concerned with your fees. They're willing to pay almost any price to work with you.

COMMODITY VERSUS TRUSTED ADVISOR

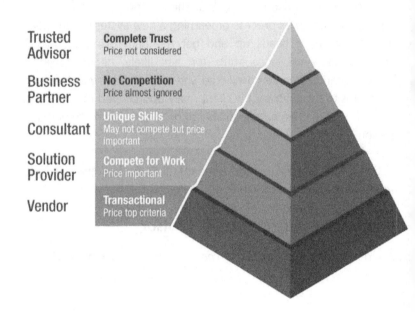

Vendor

The vendor relationship is transactional. The client is interested in hiring you for a specific purpose and price is the main factor in their decision. There is little opportunity to build a relationship as a vendor. The client considers you a commodity – does not see any difference between you and any other provider, and you must compete on price to win work.

Solution Provider

Clients will hire a solution provider to solve a particular problem. It is a focused relationship and rarely goes beyond solving a specific problem. Price is still a key factor in selecting a solution provider as well as their ability to accomplish a specific limited project. Getting work as a solution provider is often a competitive process.

Consultant

A consultant usually has expertise in a specific area of business or technology and is often hired to solve a range of problems or work for a client in an ongoing basis. When hiring a consultant, a client is especially concerned about their credentials and experience, and price may be a secondary factor. While consultants often get repeat business from a client, they may still have to compete for work on occasion, or face price scrutiny.

Business Partner

When you reach partner status with a client, you are often given work without price being a significant factor. A partner is a consultant that the client trusts very much and shares confidential information with. In some cases, the trust level is so high, the partner may be treated as a member of the client's inner circle, executive team or board member.

Trusted Advisor

A trusted advisor is the pinnacle of client relationships. A client will treat a trusted advisor as a confidant, and price is not a factor in the relationship. A trusted advisor will often be asked to consult on areas outside of their expertise, and help a client solve their most pressing problems. They may even become personal friends.

I define a trusted advisor as a consultant that puts their client's goals and needs above their own and has proven through long term investment in their client-consultant relationship that they can be trusted in every situation.

It is not always easy to become a trusted advisor. Clients are skeptical and will keep you at arm's length until they feel real trust.

Ironically, what often builds trust is telling a client no or that you do not have an answer. Charles H. Green, MBA, co-author of the best-selling book *The Trusted Advisor* and founder of Trusted Advisor Associates relates this story:

> *"I was a newly promoted manager in a consulting firm, on my first sales call. My boss, the office EVP, accompanied me (which I resented at the time, but as you'll see quickly came to appreciate). After the usual pleasantries, the client leaned in across the desk to me and said, "Tell me, Mr. Green, what experience do you have doing marketing studies for industrial consumables (by which he meant sandpaper, their product)?"*
>
> *I knew I'd never done a sandpaper marketing study, and was pretty sure no one in our firm had done one either (after all that's a pretty narrow market), but my mind raced trying to come up with the best tap-dance version of "not exactly, but..." I could conjure. To no avail. I sat there like the proverbial deer in the headlights.*
>
> *And that's when my boss spoke up. "None that I can think of," he said, and paused. "What else would you like to talk about?" I nearly choked. Surely that could not be the right thing to say in such a moment.*
>
> *But it was. The client leaned back in his chair and laughed, saying "That's OK, hardly anyone's done sandpaper marketing. What else have you got that might be relevant?" And we proceeded to have a lively and productive conversation.*
>
> *In retrospect, what my boss did was to speak the truth. Which, ironically, was perhaps the most credibility-enhancing thing we could have said; after all, who's going*

to doubt you when you say you don't know something?

But it was more than that too. It showed that we (well, my boss anyway) had the courage required to be a truth-teller, even if it meant that we might not get the job. And being a truth-teller is a pretty good thing to be. Ultimately it meant he was putting the client's needs over our own, which again ironically is a pretty good way to succeed. By not making the sale the goal, but rather a possible byproduct of simply behaving in the client's best interest, he ensured the best outcome for the client, and (as it turned out) a pretty good outcome for us as well."

Becoming a Trusted Advisor

While becoming a trusted advisor is difficult, it is possible with an intentional approach. Besides showing clients your integrity, reliability, and competence, trust is built over time and requires a strong commitment. Your client must know you care and always operate in their best interests.

One criticism I hear a lot from clients that hire expert consultants is that they do not listen enough. Becoming a valued advisor is often more about listening than talking. When you are talking, you are not learning more about how to help your client succeed.

Another important aspect of being a trusted advisor is to be involved in many aspects of your clients' business. By helping them improve different areas of their business, beyond your immediate project work, will help them see you as a bigger asset and essential team member. One way to this is to share relevant information and make valuable introductions you know will help them with a problem they are experiencing.

I often have clients call me about topics that I was not engaged to work on. Clients will retain me to present at their management meetings or present to their board of directors. I often get asked to review strategic plans, marketing initiatives, process improvement projects, and provide input for system transition decisions. When clients know you well, they will reach out with varied requests and leverage your knowledge of their business and industry to solve other problems.

If you are interested in strategically positioning your firm or an individual to be a trusted advisor for one or more clients, learning about their business will help you get deeper into helping them achieve their crucial goals. Here are open-ended questions you can explore with them and their team members to dive deeper into what they care about most:

- What is changing in their business/agency because of Covid? (Hint: everything)
- What is their biggest challenge this year?
- What other consultants are they working with?
- What other problems are they working on?
- What are their goals for the next two years?
- What else do they need help with?
- What is causing them deep stress and anxiety?

Ultimately, being a trusted advisor is about adding a great deal of value to your clients. By ensuring they get a return on investment, you are making your team invaluable to them. If you are solving a huge problem or removing pain or anxiety from their life you will be a valued resource.

On an individual level, getting to know your clients more deeply is extremely valuable. Joel Carson, Executive Director of the GeoProfessional Business Association (https://www.geoprofessional. org/) has these tips for connecting with clients professionally and personally:

"Build extraordinary relationships with clients. Get to know your client better than anyone else. I mean really get to know them."

Professionally:
- *Fully develop an organizational chart for the client. If you cannot write it down, you don't understand the organizational structure.*
- *Meet key decision makers at all levels of the organization.*
- *Match your employees with different levels of the organization. Introduce your CEO to the client CEO. Introduce your billing manager to the client finance manager. Etc. (i.e. the zipper concept)*
- *Understand what drives business decisions.*
- *Understand how client employees receive accolades and promotions.*
- *If publicly traded, purchase one share of stock so you receive quarterly reports.*

Personally:
- *Meet for lunch, golf, social events.*
- *Connect on social media, especially LinkedIn*
- *Find out their hobbies.*
- *Learn about their families.*
- *Send them birthday cards.*
- *Write personal notes when appropriate.*

Do not rely on your memory for the items above. Build a client playbook through a Client Relationship Management (CRM) system to capture all this information."

Some of the best relationships I have had with clients became friendships over time. Mixing business and personal lives can be wonderful or dangerous. I have had staff members who got too close to clients and when things went downhill, the client leveraged their confidential information to throw them under the bus. That being said, a few of my closest friends started out as clients who viewed me as a trusted advisor.

The Race to the Bottom

Vendor relationships are a true commodity and should be avoided at all costs. Most professional service providers are at the solution provider or consultant level with most of their clients. At the solution provider level, when you are still competing for work, prices get driven down because of market forces and lack of differentiation.

As a consultant, you can charge more because of your reputation and unique experience. The difference is that you may still have to compete for work, and your fees will still be a real consideration. At this level, it becomes increasingly important to sell your value. As soon as you get into detailed discussions about your fees, you have lost the battle.

Mark Hunter, author of the best-selling books, "High Profit Selling" "High Profit Prospecting" and "A Mind for Sales", has this to say about pricing too low:

> "When you attract people who are buying because of your low price, they'll stick with you as long as you have a low price, and they'll complain about everything. This is especially true in the B2B environment. Cheap customers are whiners. People who are willing to pay more are less likely to be whiners because they know they're investing more, and they understand the value of what you're selling.
>
> Selling on low price has you swimming in the gutter of mediocrity with customers who don't understand value.

One of the amazing things I've seen is when companies take a product or service and begin to price it higher than they previously had — and they have far fewer complaints and issues from their customers. Even if the quantity they sell goes down, their bottom-line profit is far greater. Plus, they now have customers who are easier to deal with."

If you are not at the partner or trusted advisor level, your clients will try and push your fees down. They may ask you to lower your billing rates or do some work for "free."

Many consultants have incorporated business practices that drive their fees down instead of up. For example, I have seen many of my clients create a fee estimate and then lower it, thinking they need to be "cheaper" to win. Without a strategy or approach to sell on value, it will be challenging to become a partner or trusted advisor, and to raise prices.

There are some people in the A&E industry working to stop the commoditization of their services. My colleagues at the GeoProfessional Business Association (GBA) call it the "Race to the Bottom" and have recently created an initiative to elevate the profession of Geotechnical Engineering. It is a systematic problem across the industry and one that is bringing down the value of A&E firms each year.

Kurt Fraese, L.G., President, Fraese and Associates, Inc. is the co-founder and leader of an Elevate the Industry initiative. As part of the initiative, a web site was created with an accord based on guiding principles, to start to get the industry to agree to a way to value the work of Geotech Engineers. Kurt is urging everyone in the industry to sign the accord, and has this to say about the way the geotechnical profession is undervalued in particular:

The value of the geoprofessions is misunderstood and under-appreciated by clients, our communities and sometimes even among peers. GeoProfessional practitioners, their clients and the general public do not recognize the inherent value of the profession often enough, or to a sufficient degree, commensurate with the benefits derived. It is time to do more to be recognized and alter the course of both perception and reality. As a first step, join a growing number of GeoProfessionals and SIGN THE GEOPROFESSIONAL VALUE ACCORD by scanning the QR code below. Signatories to the non-binding Accord simply share a desire to achieve the mission and value proposition through the framework of its guiding principles described on the site."

Creating a Value Culture

I have found that great employees can overcome bad processes and systems. But great processes and systems cannot overcome bad employees.

Uncovering and designing your Winning Advantage is not enough. You must also galvanize your team and make value part of your DNA.

To consistently deliver value, your entire team must embrace the value message and use it to fuel their reason for going to work every day. This will also make them proud and want to work and stay at your firm.

Making your true value part of your values and a core purpose for existing will transform your culture. Your success is based on thousands of small behaviors every day that culminate in your project and financial results. Without this focus on delivering value, your staff will focus on getting the job done as quickly as possible.

If employees don't share your values or practice them daily, your results will be inconsistent. Your business processes and policies are there for a reason. They help ensure quality control, safety, accuracy of timesheets, invoices and reports, submission of project deliverables and compliance with regulations. Without adherence to these processes, your firm would have chaos.

Business education can help your employees understand why your processes and policies are important and keep them more committed to following them. All your important processes are part of the value you offer to clients – ensuring they get the results they were promised.

To create a value culture – one focused on delivering client value above the technical aspects of the project – requires a commitment to train and develop your staff. Without this kind of direction, if 100 staff were asked to complete a task, it is likely you would get 100 different results. Without the guidelines, training and consistent messaging about value, your staff will be left to deliver results based on their own interpretation and understanding.

Marketing and Sales Messages

Your UVP will become your guiding light in creating your marketing messages. Consistency of clear value-based marketing messages over time will start to become memorable to your staff, clients, and business partners. This kind of messaging will differentiate you. Your messages will be based on your UVP and your Proprietary Process.

Good marketing messaging designed around your UVP and Proprietary Process will convey your Winning Advantage. The key to a great marketing message is talking about benefits, not features. Your competitors are not good at this which can give you a huge advantage, if you can incorporate it into your culture. Your value-based marketing messages will shine where others fall short – by making you stand out in a sea of similarity and vague brand promises.

Here is an example of two architecture firms – one that is better at describing their unique value, and one that is not. The Value Architects speak with more specificity, not assuming the client can read between the lines. Which one would you feel most confident hiring to design an office building in an urban city location?

Value Architects	Qualified Architects
Our beautiful and distinctive designs avoid construction problems and ensure long-term savings in maintenance costs.	Our designs are distinctive and beautiful. We've won awards and been published in *Architecture Magazine*.
We save you millions in the construction process by selecting the right materials, monitoring the construction process, and producing drawings that are easy to build.	We provide construction administration services to ensure your building is built according to our drawings.
We manage the permit process, subcontractors and construction to ensure we hit your deadlines.	We manage the design process to keep your project on schedule.
We stick to your budget and avoid change orders by understanding your needs, communicating often, and helping you get the results you want.	Our prices are fair and transparent.
We design a sustainable, energy efficient building that will save thousands in energy costs over its life.	We use sustainable design practices and are LEED compliant.

Although the differences in the message are subtle, they focus on the client outcomes rather than the service being delivered, or the aesthetic features and awards the design firm is proud of. Subtle differences in language can produce a radically different meaning. Industry words should be avoided as they can be confusing and or detract from your message.

Jen Newman, FSMPS, CPSM, Co-founder of Elevate Marketing Advisors (https://www.elevatemarketingadvisors.com/) says this about how important it is to differentiate your marketing message:

> *"A/E/C firms often struggle to distinguish themselves from their competition. Differentiation means different, however, most firms don't understand how to define what makes them unique. We are on time, and on budget – good for you, this is the bare minimum your clients and prospects expect. We are the best – prove it. We are full- service – so what, why should the client care?*
>
> *Successful differentiation is the foundation of great key messaging. It cuts through the noise and grabs the attention of your target audience to help you connect, influence, and motivate action. Well-written differentiation messaging is compelling, authentic, demonstrates value, and tells a story in a clear and memorable way. Effective differentiation messaging begins (sentence one) with a clear overarching core message followed by supporting information or 'proof points' to validate the core statement.*
>
> *To beat the commoditization game and attract ideal clients and talent, firms must RAISE their value by identifying – and then demonstrating – how they stand out amongst their competition."*

Getting your new messaging out into the world will take an investment of time and money. Marketing is a many-to-one effort that should be designed to attract your ideal client. The messaging must be consistent, clear and focused. Too many different strategies or messages will dilute your value promise and create confusion. The 5-Step RAISE Your Value Formula will prescribe the exact steps you can take to create your Winning Advantage messages and plan.

Flint McGlaughlin, founder and managing director of MECLABS, makes the strong point that a good marketing message must have clarity.

> *"The marketer's art is not persuasion; it is clarity. Indeed, when the marketer represents an authentic value proposition, clarity is persuasion."*

So, what is clarity? It is knowing your client so well that your message speaks directly to their most important values and priorities. They feel like you are speaking directly to them.

When I published my first book, *Find the Lost Dollars,* in 2013, many new clients expressed an interest in working with me. Dozens of them told me that they thought I must have been hiding in their office and had written the book specifically about them. When you know your client that well, they will feel it.

Mike Trotta, CEO at LSA, an environmental consulting firm based in Irvine, CA, recounts:

> *"In July of 2018, after our Executive Team at LSA read June Jewell's book, Find the Lost Dollars, we felt like it was a case study about our firm. We were able to identify with many of the culture traps and see where money was leaking in all nine areas of our business described in the book. We then attended the webinar, Getting Employees to Think Like Owners and as a team, became very motivated*

to explore how to train our employees to think like owners – and why not – we are a 100 percent employee-owned company.

After meeting with June Jewell and exploring our business goals, we realized that investing in a complete Enterprise approach (i.e., training all 200+ of our employees on the Find the Lost Dollars business management training program) was the best way to get all staff on the same page and focused on finding lost dollars. Along with June Jewell, we identified the following goals:

- Bring all Principals to agreement with needed business management improvements.
- Increase project profit margins by elevating project manager skills and performance.
- Assess business practices and make improvements to processes and systems.
- Transform our culture to be more business focused.
- Increase fees and focus on getting clients and projects that are more profitable.
- Implement and empower employees to be more confident in business development.
- Implement positive measures to hold employees accountable.

Our first initiative was to launch the Find the Lost Dollars Business Management Assessment, which helped us identify strengths and weaknesses in nine areas of the business. It gave our employees a voice in guiding our direction and we received hundreds of suggestions for improvement as a result.

Next, our principals group completed the training by combining the Find the Lost Dollars online courses with *weekly group discussions. Then we expanded the training to project managers and emerging leaders over the following 18 months. Through this process, we were able to establish several major initiatives that we had previously not been able to identify, including:*

- *Daily timesheet entry by all staff.*
- *Only working on projects that have a signed contract.*
- *Holding weekly project budget and profitability report reviews.*
- *Updating our standard contract terms.*
- *Updating our estimating templates.*
- *Getting retainers up front.*
- *Decrease write-offs from scope creep.*
- *Adding contingencies to budgets*
- *Cost recovery for subcontractors and vendors.*

These initiatives have resulted in increasingly improving project management practices, which in turn have led to improvements in billings and cash flow. Our project managers are much more aware of managing projects to budget, getting retainers from new unknown clients, avoiding scope creep by getting change orders, and ensuring our fees are high enough to make a profit.

We will continue to train all our employees to Find the Lost Dollars so we can elevate the entire team to a high level of business aptitude. We are very excited with our results and highly recommend the Find the Lost Dollars program to architecture and engineering (A&E) firms looking to improve their financial results."

Thought Leadership

One strategy to market your UVP is to create content that educates your clients and creates brand recognition for your firm. Thought leadership is a great strategy for raising your individual and firm's visibility. It is important that your content is written specifically to appeal to your ideal clients and is positioned in a way to be educational and not sales focused.

This can be done by creating videos, blog posts and other articles, speaking at events, being interviewed by the media and being a guest on podcasts. You can also create your own podcast and interview experts in your niche markets to attract ideal clients to your content. Having your own podcast enables you to build a loyal audience and get direct access to prospective clients you don't know. It will also enable you to interview your existing clients which helps build stronger relationships and lets you highlight your project success through your clients' voices.

Increased thought leadership through online content will also increase organic traffic to your web site and increase your firm's site engine optimization (SEO) which makes it easier for people to find you in Google and other search engines. Having videos on YouTube also has this effect because YouTube has become one of the largest search engines, and Google owns YouTube, so they give preference to popular videos on that platform.

Raising your thought leadership will require you to have a strong marketing plan and be actively engaged in social media and other marketing channels to get your content in front of your ideal clients. It is a long-term strategy that may not have immediate impact. Creating content and building your audience can take years. Many firms get discouraged by this and slow down or completely stop creating content after a year or two because of the level of commitment required to implement this strategy.

Array Architects has been extremely successful with thought leadership. They are well known in the healthcare design space due to this strategy which has given them a Winning Advantage. Their tag line and UVP is *"We are not architects who do healthcare. We are healthcare architects."*

In 2016, their former CEO, Carl Davis determined the commoditization of architecture in their healthcare niche had become too competitive which was driving down fees. Carl and his executive team developed a thought leadership strategy driven by healthcare content that would attract their ideal clients to them instead of having to compete on price. Carl's innovative approach to elevating his firm's stature required a strong commitment to developing content and marketing his firm's unique approach. They also created a healthcare advisory practice focused on helping their healthcare clients tackle other critical issues they saw impacting their clients' success. These new services include strategic planning, data analytics, market analysis and demand forecasting that go way beyond design services and put them in front of ideal clients they otherwise would have had to compete to work with.

This quote from Carl is from a blog post on their site from 2016 and explains why they took this approach to raising their firm's perceived value:

> *"Design firms must be willing to disrupt their practices to create new services and perspectives, driving the value propositions that clients need, to help move them from fee-based to value-based decisions. Until we articulate and demonstrate those differentiating value propositions, we should expect margins to erode.*
>
> *Unless we seek innovation that our clients recognize as having impact on their value chain, we should anticipate that we will be unable to drive margin growth and attract the expertise necessary for a growing and thriving practice; and we should expect firm ownership and leadership transitions to be extremely difficult. The steps*

needed to react to commoditized markets do not come without risk, but for those brave firms that embark on the mission, the rewards make it worth the effort."

Source: https://blog.array-advisors.com/insights/architects-and-the-impact- of-commoditization

Selling your UVP and Proprietary Process

The UVP and Proprietary Process are not just part of your marketing strategy. The real Winning Advantage is created when they are part of your business development (BD) and sales process. Having clearly defined value messages and a process that is easy to remember and recite will make the dreaded job of your seller-doers much easier and more enjoyable. Instead of fumbling around for words when asked what you do at a BD event, your team will be more confident that they are delivering a clear, compelling message that will appeal to an ideal client.

Consistency and clarity are key to an effective sales process based on attracting your ideal client. If a prospect is not your ideal client, your message will not resonate – and that is exactly what you want!

In his book *80/20 Sales and Marketing*, Perry Marshall describes the concept of "racking the shotgun." He describes two men in a bar in Las Vegas, and one of them racks the shotgun under the table. 80% of the people in the room have never heard a shotgun and ignore the sound. 20% know exactly what the sound is and turn their head to figure out who has the gun.

The point is that when you know your ideal client, you will know exactly what to say to get their attention. The rest of the people in your market, who are not your ideal clients, will not relate to your message and will ignore you.

It is imperative that your UVP and Proprietary Process are directed primarily at your ideal clients, otherwise, you will waste a lot of time and lost dollars going after clients that do not align with your values and goals. The best way to do this is to sit down with your ideal clients and dive deep into their thought processes. What words do they use? What are their top priorities? What is their biggest struggle?

This does not mean that all your clients will be your ideal clients, or that you should not work with a client that isn't in perfect alignment. But the services you offer and the prices you charge should still reflect the value you bring them, and they should recognize this.

Sales Process

Selling your value to your clients is where the rubber meets the road. A solid sales process is critical to selecting the right clients, setting your projects up for success, and demonstrating your Winning Advantage. Most A&E firms do not have a sales process, let alone one that differentiates them.

A streamlined sales process designed around how your ideal clients need and want to buy your services will catapult your firm to industry high win rates. Your sales process should answer the following key questions:

- How will we decide to move forward with an opportunity?
- Who will be responsible for each stage of the sales process?
- How will key stakeholders coordinate their efforts around marketing, business development, proposal preparation, and client relationships?
- What are the steps to be followed throughout the lifecycle of the sales process and how will we ensure they are completed?
- What are the data points that are captured and where are they stored?

- If using a CRM system, how is the data maintained and who is responsible for ensuring quality and compliance?
- What kind of reporting do we need to monitor each sales lead and opportunity, and our resulting success statistics?
- How do we monitor seller-doer activity and success and implement a measure of accountability around the sales process?

This is obviously a high-level overview of the areas that need to be considered when developing an effective sales process. Most seller-doers will need training to ensure they can be successful in this role, as it usually does not come naturally to them.

Once you have developed your Winning Advantage, made it part of your firm's DNA, and ensured that everyone can recite it by heart, it will be the core of your sales process. Every decision around pursuing clients must ensure that you can deliver on the promise of your Winning Advantage.

Unfortunately, many professionals give up their strategic advantage early in the sales process. Gabe Lett, FSMPS, CPSM, LPC a self-proclaimed marketing guru for engineering firms and author of The AEC Professionals Guidebook (https://www.theaecguide.com/), provides this sound advice about leveraging your position in negotiations:

> *"When engaged in pursuing work with a client, too many A/E professionals give away all their leverage in the business relationship. Giving away leverage means you are devaluing your position as an expert practitioner and approaching your client like a vendor.*

If you want the work more than the client wants to give you the work, you have no leverage as an expert. To keep your leverage and value, practice the following:

- *Pre-qualify a prospect rather than jumping at every opportunity.*
- *Be willing to walk away from a client who bickers over your fee.*
- *Instead of using generalized language, be specific. Use messaging that only applies to the specific client and could not be used with any other client."*

Having a strong sales process will set your firm up for success by ensuring you get the right clients and projects to begin with.

Building Confidence in Seller-Doers

In Chapter 2 we discussed the cold truth that most seller-doers don't want to sell. The rare few that excel at it rise quickly to be principals and leaders. Helping them succeed with training, role playing, and experience can markedly increase their confidence and results.

The key to a great UVP and Proprietary Process is simplicity. This is often the opposite of what most technical professionals are good at. They thrive at solving complex problems. But clients are often turned off by too much technical language and complex terminology. By creating a UVP and Proprietary Process that they can easily recount over and over, they will gain confidence and connect with clients better as they focus on outcomes and results rather than the technical process.

Many years ago, when I still owned my Deltek consulting practice, I put my entire team through a sales training program called Helping Clients Succeed. It was based on a book titled, Let's Get Real or Let's Not Play by Mahan Khalsa and Randy Illig. It transformed our firm because it provided a framework for talking to clients in a win-win manner. Everyone in our firm used the same language to describe who we are and what we do. Our messages were focused around helping clients succeed and nothing else. While it was designed for sales teams, my consultants benefited from having a consistent and strong value message to communicate with.

For example, we learned the concept of "No Guessing". Instead of assuming you know what a client wants or needs, you tell them, "I don't want to guess about what is important to you, so can I ask you some clarifying questions." With each point they make, you verify that you understand what they mean. You keep digging deeper until you are completely clear. This leads to much better understanding of your client, and better clarity around what they want and how to solve their problems.

I have now taken all I have learned from 30+ years of selling and condensed it into the 5-Step RAISE Your Value Formula. Ultimately, selling is about helping clients achieve their goals and getting the outcomes they want. When seller-doers are taught to do this, they will enjoy sales.

Another key to getting seller-doers to feel confident in the sales role is to help them connect to the amazing impact they are making on the client, the community, and the world. A&E firms add so much value to the world beyond just their clients. Having pride in this impact can motivate professionals and give them confidence in getting the sale to a close so the project can move forward.

When they genuinely believe that your firm provides more value, does a better job, and is more invested in the clients' outcomes, they will want to help you win because they will be confident your firm is the best firm to win the project.

Transforming Great Technical Managers into Great Business Leaders

Since 2014 I have trained over 1,500 A&E project managers, business unit leaders and C-Suite executives to develop their business acumen. I have repeatedly seen the enormous impact that having a solid understanding of financial principles and best practices can do for an A&E professional and an A&E firm.

If you are wondering why some employees don't do their timesheets on time, fail to follow company policies, and don't seem to understand why making money on projects is essential – it is because they don't! Without essential business understanding, your PMs will continue to discount, lower fees, and pursue projects you shouldn't win.

An example of how a lack of financial skills manifests every day in A&E firms is the amount of money wasted on pursuing projects that do not have an acceptable return on investment (ROI). Let's pretend you are pursuing a project with a

$300,000 fee. See the example below showing how fast you can end up with low or no profit.

Fee for project	=	$300,000
Probability your firm will be selected	=	50%
Net projected fee revenue ($300,000x .5)=		$150,000
Cost to produce and submit proposal	=	$ 10,000
Standard profit margin on projects	=	10%
Projected Profit = ($150,000 x .10)	=	$ 15,000
Net profit margin ($15,000-$10,000)/$300,000 = 1.67%		

Most managers and marketing staff do not go through this exercise to decide if a project is worth pursuing. Even with a higher chance of winning and lower cost of preparing the proposal, the project must be managed perfectly to produce a good profit.

There may be situations where you would choose to take a low profit project to get in the door or keep employees utilized during major economic downturns. However, I am not a fan of taking "loss leaders". They set your managers and staff up for failure, create tension between your team and your clients' team, and take away valuable resources that could be devoted to more profitable pursuits. And they rarely turn into profitable work later.

A lack of financial understanding by your staff will undermine your efforts to improve, add value to clients and increase fees. Investing in financial training for your staff will pay you back many times over. Once staff have learned foundational business principals and best practices, they will be much more cooperative and think more like an owner than an ambivalent staff member.

Two ways to get them interested in gaining business acumen are connecting firm profits to their own financial success and connecting firm profits to the mission of the firm (saving the planet, your community, etc.).

Here are just a few of the behavior changes I have witnessed from employees of A&E firms after going through business training:

- They ask better questions such as, how long a task should take, or how much is the budget.
- They do their timesheets daily instead of weekly or worse...
- They look for opportunities to streamline processes and make the business more efficient.
- They understand the importance of a project budget and why it is essential to monitor costs and hours.

- They pay more attention to the project scope and ask for change orders right away rather than wait several months or longer.
- They do not pursue projects you can't or shouldn't win.
- They understand the focus on utilization and how it impacts overhead and profits.
- They understand the importance of billing and collections and are less afraid of asking a client to pay an outstanding invoice.
- They feel more connected to the leadership team and the mission of the firm.
- They look for lost dollars and are proud when they have saved the firm money.

Employees who do not understand business will not embrace the RAISE Your Value Formula because business results are not important to them. Financial literacy is crucial to the success of your firm and your ability to implement the transformational strategy we are advising in this book.

CHAPTER 8

The Importance of Strategy and Your Values

"The essence of strategy is choosing what not to do."

- Michael Porter, Author, Harvard Business Review

We have all heard the famous Yogi Berra quote, "If you don't know where you are going, you might wind up someplace else." Yet many firms are operating without figuring out where they want to go.

Developing a strategic plan will help guide your firm forward. Unfortunately, many firm executives get together for a strategic planning session every year or two to map out the objectives for their business for the near- and longer-term future. Then they go back to their "day job" and get sucked back into the details of their projects and clients and don't execute.

Without a sound strategy, your employees will not have the guidance to steer them in the direction the leadership team wants to go. They will continue to let the usual culture traps guide their decisions and behaviors.

Another scenario I see too often in A&E firms is that they have a strategic plan but either aren't using it to guide decisions and daily

Behaviors, or worse, ignore it completely. Going away once a year to focus on your business is not enough. To effectively implement a strategic plan, there needs to be regular review, monitoring of progress, and accountability for implementing key initiatives. Being busy is not an excuse for failing to do so.

If you have a plan and are making real progress against it, congratulations! My suggestions in this chapter will help bolster what you already have by adding a value component to your goals.

Most of us have gone through one or more recessions in our careers. In my case, five. It is inevitable that we will face another at some point. I believe all firms need to operate as if an economic downturn is around the corner. This means bolstering your client relationships, controlling cash, ensuring your projects are profitable, and having a strategy that enables you to thrive in bad times.

It is usually advisable to engage a facilitator to help your leadership team get through the strategic planning process successfully. Ray Kogan, AIA, Kogan & Associates, in his book, *Strategic Planning for Design Firms*, describes the value of having a facilitator to help you with your strategic planning:

> *"Strategic planning retreats work best when they are facilitated professionally. The facilitator— optimally a strategic planning consultant—keeps the group focused on mission, vision, issues, goals, strategies, and action plans, and also—because he or she under-stands the industry— knows when and how to ask the kinds of provocative questions that will keep the group thinking strategically. The facilitator will also give the group a reality check, noting that the firm may be embarking on a path that has caused problems for other design firms."*

As Ray points out, hiring a facilitator with knowledge of your industry is a key to leveraging outside experience and bringing in new ideas.

What Goes into Developing a Strategy?

Strategic plans take many shapes, sizes, and formats, but there are essential elements that all plans need to drive success. Most strategic plans include evaluation of one or more of the following elements:

Defining Your Mission, Vision, and Values (MVV)

Every strategic plan must address the mission, vision, and values of the leaders. These are the guiding principles for the firm and incorporate the dreams, passions, and ambitions of the owners and leaders. The mission states the purpose of the organization, the vision states a bold dream for the future, while the values set expectations and boundaries, guide the behavior of employees, and are a guiding light for clients and partners you do business with.

It is critical to your firm's success that you figure out your purpose, your goals for the future, and what you stand for.

Defining your MVV gives your employees, clients, and partners a clear way to talk about your firm with stakeholders and a way to differentiate your value. If you do not give them clear talking points, you have no idea what they are saying.

Many firms schedule an executive retreat, create their MVV, proudly share it with their teams, and then don't discuss it again until their next business planning season. Most employees (including leaders) would not be able to share their understanding of your MVV when asked.

Your mission should give your clients and employees a way to identify why you exist as a company – your purpose for being in business. Your business should exist to make an impact and defining what that desired impact is can help clients and employees identify with your brand. For example, the mission of Gannett Fleming, a top ten ENR 500 engineering firm, is *to be a driving force in improving our communities and sustaining our world.* They do this by focusing on core values like sustainability and diversity, and inclusion that make the world a better place.

Your vision gives your team something to strive for. To be the best, biggest, most influential firm in your market, or the world, is something you can rally your team to get behind. It should be motivational and inspiring. Very often your vision remains internal and is used to fuel growth and inspire employees. Your values are your guiding principles and commitment to what is most important to your leadership team and employees. If your employees believe in your values, you will have higher performance and success. If they do not, or you don't practice your stated values in real life, you will lose employees and find it difficult to build a cohesive and high-performing team.

An example of this is a 50-person engineering firm that hired us to investigate why they had higher than average turnover. When we talked with their employees confidentially, we discovered that the firm leadership was constantly preaching their core value of respect, yet they continued to engage with nasty clients that treated their employees disrespectfully. The leadership was aware of this treatment but did nothing about it because these clients brought a lot of revenue into the firm.

Inconsistency is very apparent to employees and why they often dismiss leadership efforts and messages.

Your company's values should be shared frequently both inside and outside of your firm. They should be on your recruiting sites, in marketing messages, social media, web pages, proposals and even email signatures. They should be your guiding light for client communications, client selection, hiring, and key business decisions.

I was at a recent business meeting with a group of A&E firm leaders, and only two of 15 could cite their firm's values. If you don't know your values, neither do your employees. You effectively don't have any.

Every employee should be able to recite your core values. Developing an acronym for your core values can help everyone embrace and remember your core values.

I have three core values that have driven my work and businesses for over 30 years.

- Deliver measurable results that meet our clients' strategic goals and objectives.
- Care about people.
- Leverage the best technology to ensure maximum efficiency and financial success.

For a long time, I lived and breathed these values without giving them a name or having them in writing. I have preached behaviors such as *Always do what we say we will do*, and *Treat employees and clients according to the Golden Rule* that help drive the behavior of our employees. When hiring employees, it was always important to us that our employees embraced these values and lived them every day.

Failure to align your firm's values with those of your clients and employees can cause problems including bad behavior, turnover of clients and employees, failure to follow company policies, ethical and legal concerns, and disputes about how to handle unexpected issues. Strong values will define your culture and what you stand for.

SWOT Analysis

This is an analysis of your current strategic position in terms of your strengths, weaknesses, opportunities, and threats. It gives you a way to evaluate what is going well, what needs improvement, and the current market situation you are operating in.

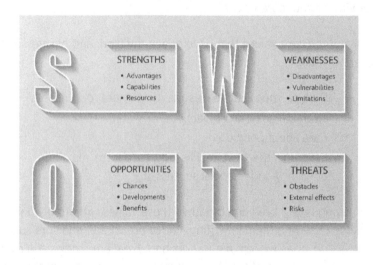

Visit www.aecbusiness.com/RAISEYourValue/Resources or scan the QR code below to download a sample SWOT analysis form.

Get Your Resources

Feedback from Employees, Clients, and Partners

Part of your strategic planning process should also include asking your employees, clients, and business partners (subcontractors, key vendors and consultants) about how things are going from their perspective. This can provide valuable feedback to influence where to take your company. Your valued clients, employees, and associates can provide a unique outlook and much needed shot of reality, as well as some potentially new ideas you had not previously considered. It will also have a key benefit of garnering buy-in to your new strategy.

Market Research

It is critical to understand the environment for the markets, industries, and geographies that you are planning to operate in. This research should include trends, key clients, competitors, economic data, and other factors that determine success.

Competitive Analysis

It is important to compare your services, strengths, and results against competitors. Knowing your competitors and gaining intelligence around their strengths and weaknesses can help you develop an effective value proposition, marketing messaging and differentiating sales strategy. We will look at some ideas below for evaluating your SWOT against your competitors.

Financial Analysis

Numbers do not lie and are a critical tool in creating an effective strategic plan. Looking at your firm's historic key performance indicators (KPIs), benchmark analysis comparing your firm's metrics to others in your industry, trend analysis over time, and a detailed breakdown of your KPIs by clients, type of client, markets, type of projects, and business units can provide valuable insight into areas where you may want to expand or contract your business focus.

Strategic planning should answer the following questions, which will enable you to develop an annual marketing plan, one- and three-year goals and objectives, and annual budget:

- What is our exit strategy or longer-term end goal for ownership transition? If your goal is to have your younger managers eventually become principals and buy out the current owner's interest, you had better allow 8-10 years to get everything in place or find an alternative transition plan. If your plan is to sell, focusing on business processes, backlog and profits should take center stage.
- How much revenue and profit do we want, or expect, to generate in both long and short-term increments (5 years, 2 years, 1 year, etc.)?
- Who is our ideal target client and how will we find them? This includes looking at the industries, geographies, size, demographics, and type of client (public versus private) that you will pursue. You may need to have a different ideal client profile for each of your business units/markets.
- What services will we offer?
- What types of contracts will we pursue?
- How many people will we need to hire (or let go) to achieve our expected goals? This is also driven by determining if you have the right talent to achieve the goals you are setting.
- What will be our primary methods of acquiring new clients?
- Should we consider an acquisition as part of a strategic initiative to move into a new market, or offer new or expanded services?

All these questions, and possibly many others, are critical to getting and keeping your team focused, and achieving your firm's strategic goals and objectives. Developing this roadmap for your company's future is the critical first step to ensuring that you have set the course and are traveling in the right direction. The next step is to build the context with which you will measure your company's performance over the next year and get your employees to execute the plan.

Selling on Values

Selling on value is a framework for getting clients focused on results rather than cost. To sell on value, you must also sell on your *values.* This means ensuring that your projects, clients, and business practices align with your values.

Without a clear understanding of your values, your employees will not execute according to your plan. They will provide inconsistent service, not follow standard operating procedures (SOPs), and erode your project success and financial results.

By selling on values, you ensure your employees' and clients' values align with the company's standards and goals. You can confidently talk about your services and results when you are certain your employees can deliver on your promises.

By establishing clear guidelines for client and project selection, as well as great hiring practices, you can ensure that your firm's values are not just words on your website but a living, breathing part of your culture. The questions in your Go/No- Go process should test the client and project against your strategic goals and your values. Making sure you are on the same page with clients on quality, budget, schedule, and team will go a long way to avoiding disputes and ensuring higher profits.

One piece of advice I have for my clients when defining their values is to ensure you address two key areas – employees and money. Many firms design their values around clients and projects, and don't specifically mention employees and financial success. I believe focus on financial success should be a core value. It is in the best interest of the firm, your employees and your clients that you are a financially successful firm. Your clients also want to know they are working with good businesspeople that will manage their budgets effectively.

Finding clients that align with your values will solve issues that you may currently experience. When clients have the same values, they understand why you have the processes and policies you have and respect the way you run your business.

You can attribute almost all problems with clients to a misalignment in values. If your core values are to value your employees, good clients will also value your employees. If your core values ensure work/life balance for your team, good clients will not ask your employees to respond to their emails every night and weekend. If your policies require approval for change orders before proceeding with extra services, your good clients will not ask your employees to break the rules or try and get work for free. If your clients share your values, they will take your advice and not try to take shortcuts or break rules against your recommendations.

It is much easier to sell on value instead of price when you have a good client that shares your values. If you want to make life easier for yourself, your team and your business, only work with good clients that align with your core values.

How Do You Rank Against Your Competition?

Understanding your competition is essential to differentiation. Competition changes over the years so it is important to do a competitive analysis on an annual basis as part of strategy planning.

The purpose of competitive analysis is to understand why you are winning and losing. It can help guide your strategy, differentiate your marketing message, and look for "blue ocean" opportunities.

Evaluating competitors can also be motivating if you are growing and able to track progress against other firms in your industry and geographies. If you have many offices, disciplines, and market sectors, a competitive analysis can be a daunting exercise.

There are many resources that can help you determine who your competitors are and how you compare to them. The following are some areas to garner intelligence about your competitors. Chances are you know most of your competitors. The ones you lose to the most are your biggest threats. If you have moved into new geographies or markets, you may need to do more analysis.

Once you have determined who your key competitors are, you can evaluate the following sources to gain valuable insight about them:

- Spend time on their web sites, LinkedIn, Google, and other social media to gather intelligence about them and how they are positioning themselves. Look specifically at their marketing messages, About Us pages, online directory profiles, and recruiting assets. Review the projects they are promoting – this can provide insight into their market strategy and strength in those areas. Also, review the quality of their web site. I often see dated web sites that give an image of "old school" rather than high-tech or cutting-edge.
- Look at what associations they belong to and how they are showing up in thought leadership in your geographies and markets. Engineers commonly network at AIA events and seeing how they advertise or promote themselves at industry conferences may be helpful to understanding their value proposition.
- Review their thought leadership by looking at videos, blog posts, advertisements, and other assets they are using to promote their authority, credibility, talent, and uniqueness.

- Interview your employees that used to work at those firms to uncover weaknesses that are not shared online (many firms fail to do this).
- Hire a market research company to help you. They have special tools to uncover elusive or otherwise inaccessible information about companies.
- Talk with consultants, CPAs, lawyers, and contractors that you work with in your industry. They may be reticent to tell you anything if they are already working with a firm, but if they aren't working with them anymore or getting information from a third party, they may have some unique insights.
- Review data from publications that rank firms in your industry (e.g., ENR 500 for engineering firms).
- Look them up on Dun & Bradstreet, www.dnbHoovers.com and other similar services.
- Go to industry conferences and talk with people. It is amazing how much people will share face-to-face that they won't share in email or on the phone.
- Do not forget to Google your own firm as well as your general service types and see what comes up. A common online practice for competitors is to tailor their Google AdWords campaign so that *their* pages show up on top if someone Googles *your* firm. Looking at your own Google listings and related pages online can be very insightful.

Performing a SWOT analysis against your competitors, as in the figure below, can be a valuable exercise. This will help you identify potential areas where your firm has an advantage that could be important to your clients.

Visit our Resources page at
www.aecbusiness.com/RAISEYourValue/Resources or scan the
QR code below to download a sample
SWOT Competitive Analysis

Get Your Resources

Having sharp competitors is not all bad. They can help drive you to be better and more creative. You may end up collaborating or teaming with them on occasion. Or like me, you may sell your firm to one of your competitors someday.

RAISE Your Value

STRENGTHS	MY COMPANY	COMPETITOR #1	COMPETITOR #2	COMPETITOR #3
Business Advantages (size, skills, service offering, geography, reputation, financial, online presence, etc.)				
Competencies				
Areas We Make the Most $				
Areas We Excel				
WEAKNESSES				
Where We Lack Resources				
Services We Don't Offer				
Areas We Don't Perform Well				
Areas We Lose $				
Areas We Need Improvement				
OPPORTUNITIES				
Beneficial Trends				
Niches Competitors Missing				
New Technologies				
New Client Needs				
New Client Problems				
National Crisis (e.g., pandemic)				
THREATS				
Obstacles To Overcome				
Aggressive Competitors				
Successful Competitors				
Negative Economic Conditions				
Government Regulations				
National Crisis (e.g., pandemic)				

Implementing Your Strategy

A strategy is useless if it is just a document that no one uses. A good strategic plan should be communicated to all employees and the core values discussed frequently. It should include an action plan with priorities, detailed tasks and assigned responsibilities with due dates.

Frequent review of progress towards goals is critical to keeping implementation of your plan top of mind. Most importantly, how you perform every day, including selection of clients is critical to achieving growth and revenue goals.

One of my clients, FAE Consulting in Deerfield Beach, Florida recently went through a strategic planning exercise. They are a small, woman-owned mechanical, electrical and plumbing (MEP) engineering firm focused on growing. CEO Ursula Iafrate believed all employees should contribute to the plan and asked her team to submit their ideas for development of the firm's mission, vision and values. Then the executive team met with a facilitator and developed their plan including areas to grow and the core values that would guide that growth.

They named their new strategic initiative FAE 2.0 and had a whole company launch party along with food, drinks, and Yeti water bottles with their core values on them. Now every team member has their firm values on their desk and those values guide key decisions, client strategies, and behavior.

Implementing your strategic plan is the hard part. It requires commitment, focus, discipline and getting buy-in from the entire team. The goal of this book is to help you develop and implement a plan that will transform your business.

Getting buy-in for your strategic plan is critical to its success. Taking a bottom-up approach, as Ursula did at FAE, is critical to having all your employees feel like it is their values and their plan. It is important to help each of them see WIIFM – *what's in it for me*. If they believe the plan only benefits the owners or elite leaders at the top, they will resent the plan and either become uninterested, or worse, sabotage it.

In order to implement their plan, Ursula hired my firm, AEC Business Solutions, to work with them monthly to improve technology, processes, project management, leadership, and pricing. We work with them consistently to ensure they are making progress and improving. In just eight months of working together, profits have doubled.

In Chapter 10, I will lay out the steps needed to develop and implement your strategic plan based on your Winning Advantage.

CHAPTER 9

Strategic Pricing

"Quality is remembered long after price is forgotten."

- Aldo Gucci

Most professional services firms do not price strategically. If the only strategy you are considering is getting a new client or winning a new project, you have put yourself at a disadvantage. I have found that many fee estimates are created from previously submitted proposals without regard if they were winners or losers.

This "strategy" is a recipe for low fees and commoditization. It fails to consider your understanding of what your ideal clients really want. Mistakenly, we assume that all clients understand our process and will buy based on the right words paired with a competitive price.

But what if your clients can't compare your services to any other firm? What if your proposal and pricing is so different, that they can only consider whether they want you or not? What if your Winning Advantage is so strong and apparent, they must read every word? Pricing can be a strong differentiator – and not just by being cheaper.

Why It Is Better to be High Priced

Many business owners and leaders are afraid to raise their prices because of fear of being rejected. Deciding to be a high-priced consulting firm will change everything about your firm and is not right for everyone. But the rewards of raising prices and pursing better clients is immense.

Having high prices automatically gives the impression of being more valuable - Charging the highest prices in your field is the opposite of a commodity – it removes the competition and makes clients desire you more, even if they can't afford to work with you.

When you are the expensive option, you will attract a different clientele - Your clients will gain status from working with you and will assume your product is better. By carving out a niche with clients that can afford higher fees, you will eliminate most of the competition and must be much more selective about the projects you are willing to take.

Clients are less cost-conscious and more focused on getting results - Your clients will be more focused on the outcomes than the price. They will be willing to pay for quality. This is especially important if you are a firm that has quality as a core value.

You will need fewer clients and projects to reach higher revenue levels - Your firm will grow faster with less effort, and you won't need to hire as many people to earn the same revenue. Your profits will be greater too.

You will be able to attract first-class employees that want to work for a well-recognized, high-end firm - Most employees want to work for a firm that is visibly better and is financially successful. Your brand will be magnified, and your list of clients will be impressive. This will provide an advantage in recruiting and retention.

You will improve your culture - Having a value message is very powerful in forming the culture of your firm. Instead of just focusing on technical or aesthetic capabilities, your team will be able to rally around the core messaging of delivering great results and outcomes. Your employees will be proud to work for a first-class firm that is the best in your field.

You won't have to change much about how you deliver services - The difference between the product you deliver now at lower prices and the product you must deliver to attract and satisfy more affluent clients is very small. In fact, by understanding your Unique Value Proposition and Proprietary Process (Chapter 7), you will be able to lower the cost of doing business by creating a scalable, repeatable way to sell and deliver your services.

Pricing Methods

Most professionals charge for their services in a combination of three key billing types:

1. **Time and Materials (T&M) or Hourly -** In T&M or Hourly pricing, services are charged and billed at an hourly rate, usually by labor category or role. Often rates are negotiated in a competitive proposal, master service agreement (MSA), or ongoing with an existing client.

While many A&E firms believe this is the safest type of pricing, it can end up being the worst. Very often the rates are based on prior year overhead rates and do not take into account rising salaries, benefits, and other indirect costs. If rates are not contracted to increase each year with an escalation clause, service providers can find they are working for minimal profits or even breaking even. In detailed analysis we have done with our clients over the past five years, we found that T&M projects were not as profitable as lump sum. In fact, lots of the rate tables we analyzed were losing money on half of the labor categories.

Another problem with hourly billing is that you can never make more than your billing rate multiplied by the number of hours charged. There is never an opportunity to charge a client more based on the value you bring or how well you manage projects.

David Stone of blüStone marketing (https://www.blustonemarketing.com/) offered me this exercise that illustrates the trap of hourly work. Think about the highest rate you have ever charged a client – for this example, we will say $300 an hour. That is your perceived value. Then think about a time when you helped a client and saved them a lot of money – let's say $100,000. This probably happens every day in your firm. That hour you charged them was worth $100,000 to them, and you were only compensated $300. Your client got a great deal! Charging an hourly rate says a lot about what you believe you are worth and creates that same impression on your clients.

The worst type of contract you can get is Hourly with a Not-to-Exceed (NTE) limit. These types of contract methods only benefit the client and cause you to lose profit if you are more efficient. Don't accept these types of contracts!

One time I had a new client call me about helping them launch a new initiative in their firm. The initiative was crucial to achieving their strategic plan and I knew I could add immense value. They stipulated they would pay me hourly with a Not-to- Exceed and asked me what my rate is. I have not done any hourly work in over ten years and do not have a billing rate. I explained this to them and told them I needed to understand the scope of the project and I would give them a fixed price. I also told them I was confident my advice would save them a lot of time and money, and I would give them a full money back guarantee if they were not thrilled. I also explained that if I had to charge them an hourly rate, it would have to be at least $1000 an hour – more than three times the rate of the executive I was talking with. They moved forward in hiring me for the project at a fixed price, and we took great care to define the scope which benefited both of us.

2. **Fixed Fee or Lump Sum -** Fixed fee or lump sum contract types are quite common in A&E projects. This contract type is used when the service provider is relatively sure about the level of effort (LOE) required to complete the project.

    Most consultants develop a scope of services that details what they are going to do, and not do, as part of the fixed fee amount. When the scope is agreed upon by both the consulting firm and the client, any changes or additions to the project scope will require an approved change order to increase the contract amount.

    This contract type can be a benefit to both the service provider and the client. Some clients prefer it as they are better able to budget and have an upper limit to what they plan to spend.

    Complications can arise with a lump sum project in the following circumstances:

- The scope is not detailed enough
- The scope omitted critical components such as travel, meetings, contingencies, etc.
- There wasn't enough profit budgeted in the fee
- The consultant did not understand the client's requirements or desired outcomes
- The contract language failed to set expectations about approval for change orders
- The proposal did not address handling of unexpected but potentially damaging situations such as natural disasters, turnover on the project team, extensive delays in the project, disputes, regulatory issues, etc.
- The client provided a contract with onerous terms and conditions and unrealistic requirements
- The consultant severely underestimated how long it would take to finish the project
- The consultant fails to manage the project within the budget and schedule
- Employees working on the project are not aware of the scope, schedule and budget, or not paying attention.

3. **Cost Plus Profit Percentage (Cost Plus Fixed Fee for Government Contractors) -** Cost Plus or Cost-Plus Fixed Fee (CPFF) contracts are normally used for federal government contracts. This type of contract is similar to T&M except the hours are billed at each employee's raw labor cost and burdened with benefits, overhead and a fixed profit percentage. These types of contracts are often audited to ensure that the government is being billed fairly and the overhead rates used are accurate.

   These types of contracts can be burdensome to the consulting firm by requiring extra accounting processes, more accurate tracking of costs and more diligent timesheet practices. You can also lose profit by having too low an overhead rate or if some of your overhead is deemed nonchargeable. This type of contract can be the most restrictive with less net profits.

Most government agencies are limiting profits on CPFF contracts to 8% to 10%. If you have a lot of public projects, you may need a volume of work with dedicated resources to be profitable.

Alternative Pricing Strategies

Most consulting firms have a specific way of pricing their services and continue to do it the same way year after year. Proposal templates are used repeatedly for similar projects. Using boilerplate language and standard rate tables does not leverage the 80/20 rule and consider clients willing to pay for different outcomes.

Years ago, as a Deltek software reseller, we realized there were certain clients that wanted hand holding through the software implementation process. They were willing to pay more to guarantee a faster or smoother implementation. In some cases, they did not trust their employees to get the job done without a lot of extra help. We put together some options for those types of clients, and by asking the right questions up front, we knew which clients to offer our "premium" services to. This strategy alone increased our average revenue per client and improved our implementation success and client satisfaction for those types of clients.

Many seller-doers just assume a client will not pay more and never try to explore alternative pricing strategies or different offers. It can be beneficial testing different pricing methods on new clients and in some cases existing clients.

By looking at the services you provide and determining ways to make them more efficient and profitable, you can offer them on a lump sum basis and make a 20% or more profit on each project by limiting the scope and systematizing the process.

The following are some pricing methods to play with that can 2X, 5X or even 10X your contract amount for a project:

Offers

Consider optional extra services to offer clients who are looking for a specific result. You may already be performing a service that the client is not aware of and valuing. There may also be extra services commonly added to your contracts that you are frequently doing change orders for. These services can be presented in a proposal with a "special" lump sum price that has extra value to your client. You may be surprised to see your clients expressing interest or asking questions about these extra services.

This technique can be used if you have other departments that offer complementary services. Even if only one out of 20 clients is interested in it, it does not hurt to have an unrelated service offered in the proposal.

Bundles

Offer clients bundles of services together that increase the total sale amount but are of value to them. By understanding what clients want, you can include extra services as part of a bundled core service. This will enable you to ensure client satisfaction, increase your revenue, and differentiate your firm from others.

I have done this successfully by bundling my assessments, training courses, and monthly services for clients that need and want more help with implementing new business processes. I often bundle my workshops and executive coaching services in as well depending on the needs of my clients.

The key to being successful with bundles is to offer different options and test them. See what combinations your clients ask about or are most interested. I have used bundles successfully with the Good, Better, Best strategy below.

Upsell & Cross-Sell

An upsell is when you sell an additional service to your client during or after finalizing the sale. An upsell can be combined with a cross-sell to offer services from another department in your firm.

To successfully implement an upsell process, you must understand your client and what they really want. They may come to you for help with one service but ultimately need help with other parts of their projects. If you know their business, you may be able to break into other parts of their organization by discussing their needs for services outside the scope of the core proposal.

One way to upsell your clients is to include as many options in your proposal as possible. Instead of listing what is NOT included in your scope of services, make a list of all services that they may want to buy with a price or price range. Clients do not always know what they really want, and this helps them consider all the other services you could provide for them, including services from other parts of your company.

The other benefit of listing all the additional services you offer is to make it clear that they are not included in your scope. This may trigger additional questions and enable you to educate your client about your proposed services.

Good, Better, Best Packages

This is one of my favorite methods for increasing revenues and creating a new service offering for your clients. It will take creativity and require testing to figure out what will work for your specific niche but once you figure it out it can be a game changer.

To implement a successful Good, Better, Best pricing package, you must start with the minimum scope that you would offer the client to get the results they asked for. This would be your "Good" option. It is critical that the "Good" package is enough to ensure success with the client and is good enough to maintain quality, conform with your standard of care and "good" results. It is your barebones scope.

The "Better" option would be everything in the "Good" package but with added services and/or expedited results. Remember the Fast, Good, Cheap principle. The "Better" option is adding faster or more services but at a higher price. Most clients gravitate to the "medium" option so make sure you price it strategically to earn a higher profit.

The "Best" option should be a lot more expensive – way more than you believe the client will pay. It should include everything you can throw into the package. You can include the option for "unlimited" emails or meetings, unlimited design reviews or drawing changes, multiple meetings a month, reports, status updates, additional coaching or consultation with firm principals, etc. This option works best when you are a prime contractor and working directly for the owner. You can also put a timeline on it, spread the payments monthly, and include options that only these most exclusive clients get.

I do not understand why more professionals do not use this method. I have been using it successfully for years. I have used it to create a whole new revenue stream and when combined with subscriptions (below) it can have a significant impact on revenue per client.

One way for A&E firms to use this is to develop or offer a special technology that is only available as part of the "Best" package. If the client wants the benefit of that technology, they must select that option.

I recommend giving each package a special name that is related to the results you are promising. I work with an exclusive small group of special "Enterprise" clients that get special attention, unlimited training options, and guaranteed results. They are my VIP clients and benefit the most from working with us. We focus on specific goals each month and make great progress helping them achieve their most important goals. Some clients will pay more to have guaranteed results, extra attention, and the support and accountability that comes with an extended program.

You likely encounter examples of Good-Better-Best pricing daily. Outside of professional services, it is widely used. You may be thinking this strategy is impractical, or worse, embarrassing. But if created tastefully and presented to a client in a way that shows you are trying to help them get what they want, you might find your average fees increase.

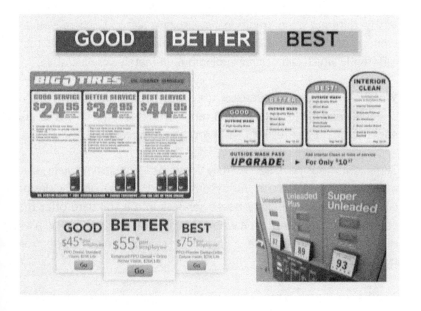

Productized Services

One way to get a different group of clients that needs your help but is looking for a more cost-effective solution is to productize your expertise. This can be done with a book, workshop, coaching program, training program, mastermind group or even a software app that solves a specific problem in your industry.

An example would be a long-time client of mine from my Deltek days, Aerosol Monitoring in Hanover, MD. They took the expertise they had in hazardous chemical abatement and remediation, safety and other skills, and developed training courses to teach these skills. It has become a major part of their revenue and business model and has led to other partnerships and projects.

It is often easier to offer packaged services in a group for clients that need a similar result. Selling these types of productized services is vastly different than traditional consulting services where you are working with one client. You will need to learn how to market them differently which can be challenging but ultimately very lucrative.

When services are productized, they are easier to implement with a scalable repeatable process and more predictable results. It is also easier to guarantee results (see below about guarantees).

Some A&E firms have successfully converted standard services, such as 3D imaging, Matterport, model design, web design, graphic design, GIS and similar technology-based services into a standard offer that can even be purchased on a web site. Using technology can be a big differentiator and provide a lucrative revenue stream aside from traditional services.

Another approach is to develop a mobile app that solves a problem a client has. Investing in technology can be risky, so having the right people, planning, and managing the development and sales of software products is critical.

Subscriptions

Subscriptions are a fantastic way to create recurring revenue streams. They can be used for many different applications including the productized services and bundled services referenced above. They are usually services that are offered weekly or monthly and have a defined scope and promised results.

I have had clients that created separate income streams with subscription-based services including environmental monitoring, facility management, and other kinds of maintenance. Some design firms, such as Nelson, have expanded their services into many different areas including traditional marketing agency type work such as branding and communications design. This type of work can be contracted as a retainer or subscription type of fee, charging the client monthly for regular services.

The key to selling services as subscriptions is to have effective processes that ensure stellar results. By getting impressive results for clients in a repeatable and predictable way, you can easily get annual renewals and attract even more clients to sign up for subscription services. Having your Proprietary Process built around a repeatable and valuable result for clients can enable you to offer new and different services utilizing subscription pricing.

Having a good percentage of your annual revenue in regular predictable income streams will increase the value of your firm significantly. This method will also enable you to grow exponentially without adding more headcount. If you are considering selling your business someday, having a percentage of your revenues as subscriptions can increase your sale price multiple by 200% to 500%.

Adding Guarantees

The ultimate differentiator is a full money back guarantee. A guarantee removes all the risk for your clients and places the risk on you.

I offer an unconditional guarantee on all our training services. I have never had a client come back and ask for their money back. That is because I ensure our clients see a significant, measurable ROI from working with us.

To successfully offer a guarantee, you must select high integrity clients that are committed to getting results. If you cannot guarantee the results you promise, including excellent client service, then do not offer a guarantee.

Guarantees can be creatively formulated and do not have to be unconditional. They should be created strategically so they help ensure your success. When your client performance or contribution is critical to getting the outcomes they need, it is essential to put conditions on the guarantee that ensure they follow through.

Guarantees should be based only on the conditions you can control. If you guarantee a certain deadline, but your client could delay the project, a guarantee will not work. Carefully written and agreed upon guarantees can help to ensure your client will participate in their own success and remove apprehension about working with your firm. Professionals who are confident in their ability to deliver expected results instill confidence in their clients and prospects.

If you are confident in your ability to produce results almost 100 percent of the time, guarantee offers can be effective. However, most liability insurance partners and lawyers in the A&E industry will prohibit you from using any language guaranteeing performance, quality or even service. If this is the case, look at how you can use language that does not outright guarantee results, but instills the client with confidence in your ability to deliver their desired outcomes. One way to do this is by providing case studies and references from past clients. Data about past performance such as, "we have completed over 150 successful similar projects in the last five years on schedule and budget" may be the closest you can get to offering a guarantee.

Implementing Price Increases

Increasing your billing rates or fees is critical to staying in business. Most firms increase their prices long after they should and leave money on the table. For many professionals, the fear of increasing rates often outweighs the desire to make more money.

Jeb Blount, best-selling author of several sales books including *Selling the Price Increase,* explains this dilemma perfectly:

> *"The payoff for implementing price increases without losing customers is massive! Effective price increase campaigns are far more effective at boosting topline revenue and generating profits than acquiring new customers.*
>
> *The problem is that price increase initiatives—whether broad-based or targeted to specific accounts—strike fear and anxiety into the hearts of sales professionals and account managers who are tasked with selling them to their customers. Approaching customers with price increases sits at the tip top of the pantheon of things salespeople hate to do because they fear that raising prices will reduce sales volume or open the door to competitors.*
>
> *Yet when sold effectively, customers accept price increases, remain loyal, and often buy even more."*

Overcoming fear is critical to implementing all the advice in this book. Everything is getting more expensive and price increases are critical to remaining profitable. As your costs increase, your fees must increase at the same pace or faster.

Rate increases should be planned years in advance, especially for multi-year projects. Clients should be informed about these anticipated increases so they can budget accordingly. When proper expectations are set, and price increases are regularly incorporated into your estimating and contracting process, your employees will be more comfortable dealing with client questions about rates.

Clients Don't Read Your Proposals

Taking the time to work on a client's proposal is using up valuable resources in your firm. I have consistently heard from A&E technical professionals that they are wasting too much time working on proposals. This work is non-billable and takes away from precious time they need to get their projects completed on time.

In fact, some clients do not read your proposals in detail, or at all. They scan over them and quickly disregard the ones that do not resonate. Here are some reasons as to why they may not read them including:

- Too much boring text and technical language
- Failure to focus on the clients' strong reasons for the project including desired outcomes
- They do not understand what you are offering
- Your language sounds generic or boilerplate
- You talk about yourselves too much and not enough about them
- You do not include "proof" that you will deliver
- You sound like everyone else
- They turn to the pricing page and ignore the rest
- The scope is not detailed enough
- They have more questions than answers after flipping through the pages
- They do not have time to read all the proposals submitted

This last point is perfectly illustrated with this story from David Stone, AIA, CEO of blüStone marketing:

> *"Years ago, I was working with a firm in North Carolina helping them pursue some new business with a Navy client. We took a trip up to Norfolk, VA to talk with a contracting officer about how they select consultants to work with.*
>
> *She bluntly told us she does not have time to read all the proposals that come in. They had been receiving over 50 proposals for every RFP and had to come up with a "system" to select which proposals to read and which ones to ignore. Her process was to have her assistant lean all the proposals up against white boards in the conference room and pick 12 or so to review. She based her selection on how the covers looked or whether she knew the firms. The other 38 or so proposals were disregarded."*

I find this story to be outrageous considering how much time and effort those 38 firms (and their teams) had put into those discarded proposals. If you consider the lost dollars spent on proposals that clients have never read, it is another compelling reason to only propose to clients you know value your efforts.

CHAPTER 10

Implementing the 5-Step RAISE Your Value Formula

"Thinking will not overcome fear, but action will."

- W. Clement Stone

So far, we have reviewed nine of the key principles that will enable you to uncover your firm's hidden value and design your Winning Advantage. If you have made it this far, you should be convinced that you need to stop competing on price, work with your team to develop your UVP and Proprietary Process, acquire more of your ideal clients, and RAISE your prices!

This chapter will reveal my 5-Step RAISE Your Value Formula, consolidating all the lessons of the book into an actionable process of transforming your firm to achieve remarkable results. Firms that differentiate their value can earn 2x to 10x industry standards. Combined with improved business practices and project management gained from the Find the Lost Dollars training, you can elevate your firm to the top of the industry in profits.

The 5-Step RAISE Your Value Formula is designed to be a comprehensive program to implement across your company. You can cherry pick which pieces you want to do, but ideally you should commit up to six months to do the five steps, including getting it fully implemented with your staff. This formula can also be applied in a business unit or market sector within your firm. If you have different markets you work in, you may need to go through the exercises in small teams separately.

One way we measure our clients' success implementing the 5-Step RAISE Your Value Formula is using the Value Quotient (VQ) introduced in Chapter 1. This is a free online self- assessment of how well your firm embodies the values you profess, and has created, implemented and embraced your Winning Advantage. We recommend you take the VQ Assessment *before* you start implementing the 5-Step RAISE Your Value Formula and again to assess your progress *after* you have seen some traction from it. If you are ready to get started, go to www.aecbusiness.com/RAISEYourValue/VQ or scan the QR code below and take the free VQ assessment before you start.

Take the VQ Assessment

The 5-Step RAISE Your Value Formula is based on the acronym R.A.I.S.E. explained in the graphic below:

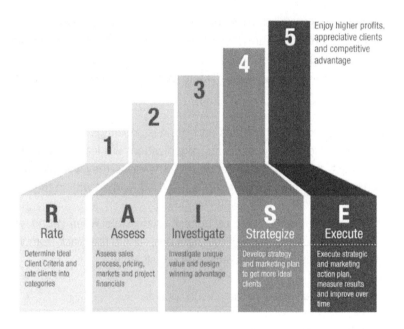

5-STEP RAISE YOUR VALUE FORMULA
Uncover Hidden Value, Design a Winning Advantage and Charge More

5 — Enjoy higher profits, appreciative clients and competitive advantage

R	**A**	**I**	**S**	**E**
Rate	Assess	Investigate	Strategize	Execute
Determine Ideal Client Criteria and rate clients into categories	Assess sales process, pricing, markets and project financials	Investigate unique value and design winning advantage	Develop strategy and marketing plan to get more ideal clients	Execute strategic and marketing action plan, measure results and improve over time

R = Rate

Step one of the RAISE Your Value Formula is to rate your current clients. When I first did this with my clients over 15 years ago, I thought it would be quick and easy. It turned out it was harder and took longer than I originally estimated. My goal is to streamline the process for you using our online tools.

Rating clients requires you to identify the most important criteria, give each criterion a weighted value, evaluate financial and other data, interview staff and quantify scores as objectively as you can. The data will be both quantitative data that is always changing, and qualitative judgements that are subjective and perhaps emotional.

Not all your employees are going to agree with the scoring system or the results. There are some clients you like very much but when scored objectively, will not rate highly.

This happened to me the first time I did this exercise with my team. My favorite client at the time, who was my first client when I started my business in 1990, ended up being a C client rather than an A client as I had presumed. I fought this rating but in the end the rating was correct.

Over time, your relationships and business dealings with clients will change. Personnel at your clients' organizations will leave, and you will have to start over with new people. In some cases, they will stop giving you projects, preferring other firms they had worked with in the past.

It is very important to be as honest as possible when rating your clients. Without real, measurable data and candid feedback from your staff, your rating will not be accurate or valuable.

Typical criteria we use to rate clients include:

Quantitative Data:

- Revenue – you can use one year, two years or last three years
- Net Revenues (total fees less subs and expenses)
- Profit Margin – expressed as a percentage of the fee billed
- Number of projects in the time period
- Days Sales Outstanding (DSO) – number of days to pay invoices
- Number of years working together

Qualitative Feedback:

- We like working with them
- Their values align with ours
- They give us great projects (as opposed to small, boring projects)
- They treat our employees well
- We use them as a reference
- They refer business to us
- We don't have to compete for work
- Level of familiarity with client's organization
- We have a close relationship with one or more key individual

I recommend developing a scoring system and weighting certain criteria higher than others. I believe being profitable should be higher than not having to compete for work. But you need to establish your own criteria based on YOUR values, not mine.

Once you have developed the list of criteria, you must do the hard work of gathering the financial data and surveying employees to get their qualitative feedback. This will take time – probably longer than you think. If you have some marketing resources to work on this project, it can get done faster depending on their bandwidth.

The scoring can be done in a spreadsheet or programmed into an app or calculated and stored directly into the client profile in your ERP system. That is how we did it – we had it programmed in our Deltek Vision system at the time to gather all the financial data, allow us to enter the qualitative scores, and it would calculate the client rating and produce reports as needed using workflows.

It is very beneficial to see these scores, and which clients end up as A, B or C clients. It will change your perspective on the value of certain clients and shock you that particular clients are better or worse than you thought. It will also cause you to think twice about how you have been treating them. When recently doing this with one of my clients, they were shocked to see they had fewer A clients than they expected.

Rating your clients allows you to then develop a plan for how to move forward with them. You may be so busy with day-to- day work that you have been ignoring your A clients. Or worse, delaying working on their projects because demanding C clients are taking all your time.

When we did this, we developed a specific plan for how to deal with each of the three categories and assigned responsibilities to both admin and billable staff based on our goals. For example, for our top ten A clients, we developed a client retention plan. The plan outlined sales goals, relationship goals, and specific actions and activities for deepening our relationship with them.

For all our clients we sent out a single question survey based on the Net Promoter Score originally promoted in the book *The Ultimate Question*. The NPS score is based on the question, "Based on a score of 1 to 10, how likely are you to recommend us to a friend." We assembled the scores from the clients that responded and compared them to the client ratings. The results were very insightful. We also had a blank text box to enable clients to leave comments. Some clients did provide comments and those were also eye opening.

For our B clients, we evaluated our work with them and employee feedback and either tried to convert them to an A client or left them in our normal client communication process.

For our C clients we had a talk, fired them, ignored them, or doubled our prices.

The main point is that you do something – especially with your A clients. It is worse to ask clients for feedback and then do nothing. Follow through and use the information to improve your services, relationships and processes. You just might see real benefits from this process including higher revenues. In any case your clients will see you care.

Make sure you take the comments to heart and make some improvements based on them. As mentioned earlier, feedback is a gift – if you do something positive with it.

Once you have finished rating clients, you will have a better understanding of who your ideal clients are and the criteria you need to assess future clients.

A = Assess

The second step of the 5-Step RAISE Your Value formula is to assess your marketing, sales, and business drivers affecting the perception of your value, both internally and externally.

This assessment will also require some deep analysis of the business practices that are driving down fees and causing you to compete on price. In this step, we will analyze the following areas:

- Marketing messages on the web, marketing collateral, and social media
- Web presence in search engines for key phrases, services areas, and markets
- Pricing practices including estimating practices, contract types, rates, proposal templates, and negotiation practices
- Internal feedback from employees about your brand, reputation, and image

- Thought leadership in specific key niches
- Business development effectiveness
- Sales process
- Go/No-Go Process
- Win/Loss rates by market sector
- Competitive analysis as described in Chapter 8
- Project profitability by market and/or geography and type of service if possible
- Client feedback about why they selected you, and how they feel about working with you.

This is a fairly comprehensive list but the specific areas to assess may be different for your firm.

Visit our Resources page at www.aecbusiness.com/RAISEYourValue/Resources or scan the QR code below to download a sample business assessment checklist you can use to do your Step-2 Assessment.

Get Your Resources

Assessing all these factors will take time. You may need help from outside to get it all done. It is important to be unbiased in your assessment of your current situation. Don't worry if the results are not stellar – they will be after we get through the five steps.

The information collected in this step will help you in Steps 3 and 4 – Investigate and Strategize.

I = Investigate

After collecting all the data and feedback from the first two steps, we are ready to start drawing conclusions and designing our Winning Advantage, composed of our UVP and Proprietary Process.

This is the fun part where your team can design and build the perfect message that will resonate with your ideal client. Then you will map out the elements of a Proprietary Process that will wow your clients.

To uncover your hidden value, you will have to dig deep into your projects. You can start with a few projects in each market or business unit, and have small groups work together to dissect projects into value elements.

Your detailed investigation of each project will include how your service, team, or design achieved the following for clients:

- Saved them money during the project
- Will save them money in the future
- Improved the viability, maintenance, and sustainability of their building
- Made them look good to their leadership, in the community or their peers
- Completed the project faster or on time
- Helped them deal with regulatory, permitting, or other obstacles
- Made their life easier by doing their job or reducing stress
- Improved the results they expected
- Avoided potential problems
- Avoided change orders that could have derailed their budget
- Exceeded their expectations
- Reduced potential risk now and in the future
- Was easier to work with

- Kept them on top of deadlines and details
- Produced a better solution than originally anticipated

Each of the value statements you uncover should be a direct benefit to the client. Try to identify as many value statements and benefits as you can for each project. Hopefully you will start to see a pattern.

An example of a value statement for a MEP engineer might be, "We saved the client over $200,000 in construction costs by designing the HVAC and plumbing system to cost less, require less space, and be easier to install." The value statement is that they saved the client money in construction. The exact benefit was over $200,000, double the amount of their fee.

Attempt to put a monetary value on every one of your benefits. The more unique and valuable each benefit is, the more ammunition you will have in designing your Winning Advantage.

Once you have completed your evaluation of where you add unique value, you are ready to develop your UVP. Your UVP should be a one or two sentence statement that answers the questions, why should I pick you, and how are you different?

Spend as much time as you can trying different UVP statements and testing them on your staff and clients, if possible. See how they resonate and whether they get any reaction. Say them out loud to see how they feel. Once the UVP is developed, your staff will say it every day in conversations, so it needs to be simple and sound compelling. Take the time to wordsmith it and get it down to the best version you can. It can always change later if needed but try and get it to a point where everyone is happy with it.

The UVP for my firm AEC Business Solutions is on the home page of our web site:

WE HELP A&E FIRMS MASTER BUSINESS AND PROJECT MANAGEMENT

Our Find the Lost Dollars online business training for A&E Firms is guaranteed to increase your utilization rate, cash flow and project profits.

LEARN MORE

A persuasive UVP for a high-end residential design firm whose ideal client is young, has a modern high-tech aesthetic, and wants to be intimately involved in the design process but has never built a home before might be:

> *"We guide you through the design process to ensure you get the modern, smart and beautiful home of your dreams and are involved every step of the way using our 5-step SMART design process."*

If your UVP sounds different than your competitors, and it is written with your ideal client in mind, it should resonate strongly with them. The more value statements you can include in your UVP, the better. If you can state who your ideal client is in the statement, it can resonate with them even more.

After you have fine-tuned your UVP, you will focus on your Proprietary Process. You can embed your Proprietary Process into your UVP as in the example above. The SMART design process is that firm's Proprietary Process.

The **SMART** acronym in this situation could stand for:

S = Sustainable – saves you money in long term energy costs and is good for the environment

M = Modern – Modern aesthetic using high quality building materials

A = Adaptable – we work closely with you every step of the way to design your dream home

R = Results – focused to ensure the design maximizes all the features and functionality you desire

T=Technology – driven smart home utilizing the latest equipment and technology

Your Proprietary Process will be a unique differentiating acronym that explains to a client what you do and how it is different. I have found it is good to start with a key word that synthesizes your UVP into a single word. This word can represent your values, but a better approach is to have it explain your project delivery process or your clients' expected outcomes in a simple and elegant way.

Because design services can be technical and complex, making what you do logical, memorable, and unique will stick out with your clients. Together with the UVP, you will have the Winning Advantage that will differentiate you in your marketing, business development, and sales process.

I shared in Chapter 7 my Proprietary Process that I created from my company name AEC Business Solutions. This acronym is already common in the A&E industry so I knew it would be memorable. And by flipping the meaning of AEC to my specific process – **A**ssess, **E**ducate and **C**reate – it is easy to remember and describe.

Another example of a Proprietary Process I developed for a 100-person architecture firm that specializes in LEED certified buildings is based on the word **DESIGN**. This client's values included being great to work with, delivering high quality, smartly designed buildings, having employees that understand business concepts (after going through the Find the Lost Dollars program), to protect a client's budget and schedule, and constructing creative and innovative designs with technology at the forefront.

DESIGN =

D = Dependable – we keep our promises and collaborate to design exactly what you want

E = Energy efficient – sustainable and LEED compliant to save energy costs and the environment

S = Superior quality – we don't cut corners and believe quality saves money in the long run

I = Innovative and creative designs that use smart technology and are highly functional

G = Guardian of your project budget and schedule

N = Nice and fun to work for and with

This Proprietary Process will only work for this firm's ideal client – an owner that wants a firm that listens, is reliable, environmentally focused, high quality, creative, will keep their project on budget and schedule and is great to work with. Combined with the right UVP that demonstrates how this approach actually costs less in the long run, this firm has a Winning Advantage every time they compete.

Once their seller-doers embraced this Proprietary Process, they were much more comfortable talking about value and differentiating their firm in the sales process.

Your Proprietary Process can embody your values, project delivery process, or what it is like to work with you. In any case, it should be developed to attract only your ideal client.

S = Strategize

This step will benefit you whether you have a strategic plan already or you don't have one at all.

To ensure your plan gets you from where you are now to where you want to be, you will need a team-focused effort to allow best ideas to be considered and ensure key stakeholders are on board. We recommend you take time away from your office with representatives from your different departments, business units, office, market sectors, or studios.

The purpose of this step is to make some key decisions about how to leverage your Winning Advantage and create a plan to galvanize your team and culture. Chances are that the work you have done in your strategic planning in the past is still valid. We are not trying to reinvent your firm or change your direction. The main goal of this step is to realize that there are ideal clients in every market you serve, and this step will help you develop a plan to pursue and win more of your ideal clients.

Your existing plan may have several of these pieces completed, and if so, you are already halfway there. You can utilize the components as they are or update them if it has been a while since they were done.

Every strategic planning consultant has their own format and there are many resources online for organizing strategic plans such as Gazelle's One-Page Strategic Plan or the Strategyzer Business Model Canvas and the Value Proposition Canvas. These are all tools I have used and subscribe to. These are excellent resources to help you organize the data into a simple plan that you can review with your employees. You can also use our Strategy Worksheet available on our resources page, a simple spreadsheet to capture the information in your Strategic Plan.

A strategic plan should draw on the intelligence learned in the first three steps along with your UVP and Proprietary Process.

Visit www.aecbusiness.com/RAISEYourValue/Resources or scan the QR code below to access the Strategy Worksheet.

Get Your Resources

The Strategy Worksheet is an Excel spreadsheet designed with separate tabs for each section. The following are descriptions of each section and guidelines for filling it out:

1. **Values** – List your values. Spend time to make sure they are clear and truly represent who you are and the types of clients and employees you want to have.

2. **Markets, Geographies, and Services** – list all the Markets / Industries, Geographies and Services you offer. Include any data gathered during Step 2 to indicate relative success of each market, geography and service type.

3. **Ideal Client Profile** – List the features and qualities of your Ideal Client. You can use the criteria you developed in Step 1 as well as any other factors you want to consider when selecting clients. You may need to develop a separate client profile for each market sector you work in.

4. **SWOT** – Analyze your firm's Strengths, Weaknesses, Opportunities and Threats. While you may have done this before, I recommend you consider updating it. If it was done before the pandemic or some other key change in your

organization such as an acquisition, change in leadership, or other significant internal event, you should review the SWOT to consider how those changes affected each category. If you have never done a SWOT before, consider getting a facilitator to help you. It can be a very valuable exercise to go through and guide some of your strategic goals.

5. **Competitive Analysis** – During Step 2 you should have developed market intelligence about your competitors. Analyze this information and enter it on the Competitive Analysis tab on the Worksheet.

6. **UVP and Proprietary Process** – Fill out the worksheet with the UVP and Proprietary Process you developed in Step 3. The strategic plan will provide the action steps to *leverage* the Winning Advantage derived from the UVP and Proprietary Process.

7. **Company Goals** – Enter your company goals if you already have a business plan. These are your high- level goals that will help you grow and take your firm to the next level. Your goals should include implementing business improvements, marketing, sales and other essential changes, such as raising your prices and revamping your sales process to pursue ideal clients.

8. **Financial Goals** – Enter your financial goals for the next year, three years, and five years. I recommend setting goals for revenue, profit and other key metrics. If you have accurate win rate metrics, the RAISE Your Value Formula should increase your win rate significantly. By implementing a better client selection strategy and revamping your Go/No-Go process your win rate could double or better.

9. **Marketing Plan** – In order to truly leverage your UVP and

Proprietary Process, you will need to adjust or overhaul your marketing. This would include writing new marketing messages, updating your web site, etc. To develop an effective marketing plan with limited resources, a good strategy is to use the 80/20 principle to figure out the 80% of your leads that come from 20% of your marketing and business development efforts.

Streamlining your marketing efforts to the most effective tactics and channels will enable you to hone your resources and get your Winning Advantage out into the marketplace to start attracting ideal clients sooner.

10. **Action Items** – Establishing action items for your highest priority goals is the key to executing the 5-Step RAISE Your Value Formula. Transforming your firm to embrace a value-based culture is a big initiative. Having specific and measurable small bite-size actions that you can implement quickly will give you traction early on.

In the next step you will prioritize your action items and create momentum around implementing them successfully.

If you have never done a strategic plan, there will be more work to do to put this together, and you may need outside help to ensure you are able to come to consensus. One of the biggest challenges many firms have is getting all their leaders on the same page. If you expect some disagreement with your key stakeholders, you may need a strong outside consultant, to lead your strategic planning efforts.

If you have already done this work before, or have a fairly recent Strategic Plan, you can use prior SWOTs, Goals, and marketing plans to create your action items. The real end product is a game plan with detailed action items that you can start to execute on. Once the Strategy Worksheet is completed, it will be a document that guides your actions, behaviors and priorities for many years.

E = Execute

The final step in the RAISE Your Value Formula is to take action. Reading this book will inspire you but if you do not follow the 5 Steps and complete your action items, you won't see any of the benefits from this program.

On the Action Items tab on the Strategy Worksheet, you should assign a team member responsibility, due date, and priority level (1-5) to each goal and action item. Most of the action items should be fairly clear, but here are some tips for ensuring they get done according to expectations:

Communicate the value and your "WHY" for implementing the RAISE Your Value Initiative with your entire team - This is important for two reasons. First, you want to make sure that team members are given the time to complete important action items. When they don't understand priorities, employees will be pulled off to work on projects and action items will not get done. Second, having buy-in from your team will help you start to build your value culture. If you have been effective at getting feedback from the very beginning, your team should already know you are working on this and want to feel that they are being heard and able to contribute.

Define all terms - Make sure every term being used is clearly defined. For example, I had a client who had a goal to become a *trusted advisor* for their top 20 clients. However, the term trusted advisor meant something different to every employee. If terms are ambiguous, you will get inconsistent or poor results.

Prioritize key initiatives - Go through all your action items with your team and rank them in terms of priority and impact. Determine which of the action items will have the biggest **impact on profits, winning work with ideal** clients, and client relationships.

Only work on two to three initiatives at a time - Most firms take on too many internal projects and never get any of them done. Pick two and get them done and then pick two more.

Create a committee for each initiative - Ask for volunteers to work on key initiatives. Create accountability around each initiative by determining how you will measure the success of each initiative.

Give detailed instructions for each action item - Don't assume your staff know what you expect or how to get started. Instructions should include the why (always first), who, what, where, when, and how to implement each action.

Meet regularly to review status - When people get busy, important non-billable tasks are discarded. The only way to keep accountability around these action items is to meet every two to four weeks to give status updates, report progress and any obstacles, and check in with the team. I have found that meeting regularly is the only way to keep these types of internal business improvement tasks on track.

Give regular team-wide status updates - Keep your employees informed about what you are doing and where you are at. Let them know the future tasks you will be working on and how it will impact them. For example, if you have an action item to train employees on the UVP and Proprietary Process, don't tell them at the last minute. Tell them way in advance so they can prepare, ask questions and voice any concerns.

With careful planning, commitment, and accountability, this process should take up to six months depending on where you are starting from. Some firms may not need to take extensive action. Others may have to start at the beginning and work all the way through development of their marketing plan, strategy, and business goals.

In any case, you will end up with a clear Winning Advantage that will attract ideal clients to your firm, enable you to charge what you are really worth, and build pride and confidence in your seller-doers to communicate the value of your firm.

I have conducted this process with over 100 firms, and in every case where the firm followed through implementing their goals, they saw significant increases in revenue, profits, and win rate.

A great example is QK based in Clovis, CA. When QK originally came to me in 2017, they had gone through a period of stalled growth following the recession in 2008 – 2010 and struggled to get back to their former size and profitability.

Our work together included assessing their business operations throughout the project lifecycle, training their key leaders and PMs, brainstorming and prioritizing goals to improve sales processes, client selection, project management, and firm administration, and developing a plan to execute on those goals.

In less than a year they had made major progress in improving business best practices all the way through their project lifecycle. Some of the changes they made included:

- Analyzed and categorized clients to determine their ideal client criteria
- Increased accountability and behavior of PMs to deliver profitable projects
- Improved estimating practices for more defined scope of services and appropriate fees
- Trained PMs to feel comfortable asking for change orders and talking about value
- Elevated client communications around value and setting expectations for results

In just the first year, they saw profits increase 4%. Realizing that not all clients are good clients has been a great lesson, which they've applied by killing the practice of offering discounts to clients that cut into profits. Their employees understand why profit is so important, and as a result, guard their project fees more diligently. This has transformed their culture and made it easier to measure and reward employees for performance.

Another great example is Banning Engineering based in Plainfield, IN. When Banning started working with us, they were looking for ways to increase fees and profits. Jeff Henson, V.P. of Operations, came to us to get his team focused on financial success, improve project management, and control scope creep.

Within weeks of starting our program, they started to evaluate project pursuits and fee estimates differently and felt more empowered to increase their fees. In just a few years their revenues have grown by over $2 million, with only adding six employees. According to Jeff, they have "knocked it out of the park." Their financial advisors are asking how they have done it – and they have attributed their change in behavior and mindset to working through our program.

I have seen this process work over and over with great success. When working with our ideal clients, we are able to guarantee increases in profits. That is because our ideal clients are committed to getting results, and we know that we can be successful working together.

This process can also work for you. I would love to see you RAISE Your Value and see the results that are possible with commitment, teamwork and enthusiasm. The only thing standing between you and leading an efficient, high-profit powerhouse that is the envy of the whole industry is taking the first step!

Next Steps

Whenever you are ready to put the RAISE Your Value Formula to work in your firm, here are three ways we can help:

1. **Take the 5-minute Value Quotient (VQ) Assessment** at www.aecbusiness.com/RAISEYourValue/VQ to assess where you are now.

Take the VQ Assessment

2. **Let's jump on a call, review your VQ Assessment results** and brainstorm how to get you some ideal clients (what fun!). We will help you determine exactly what your next one or two steps should be https://aecbusiness.com/15minutecall

3. **Join our RAISE Your Value Coaching Program** to implement the 5 Steps, find more ideal clients, raise your prices and transform your culture. In just 6 to 12 months, you will see increased profits, more engaged employees, and you and your team will be much happier working with appreciative clients that value your work.

Send me an email at jjewell@aecbusiness.com with "RAISE Your Value Coaching" in the subject and I'll get you all the details.

About The Author
June R. Jewell, CPA

June R. Jewell, CPA is a leading business expert in the architecture and engineering industry. June started working in the A&E industry in 1990 implementing the Wind2 Financial Management System and became a Deltek Premier Partner in 2005 when Deltek acquired Wind2. Throughout her career, June has worked with over 1,000 A&E firms, helping them improve their business operations, systems, and processes.

She is author of the best-selling book Find the Lost Dollars: 6 Steps to Increase Profits in Architecture, Engineering and Environmental Firms. This book has helped thousands of firm leaders, project managers, and emerging leaders to embrace business best practices and improved financial management to increase profits.

As CEO of AEC Business Solutions, June and her team provide business assessments, business coaching, training and workshops, and process improvement services to help A&E firms sell and deliver profitable projects. She is a frequent speaker at A&E industry events and enjoys finding new ways to help A&E firms succeed.

June splits her time between Reston, Virginia and Fort Lauderdale, Florida and lives with her daughter and pup JoJo. She enjoys boating, dancing, karaoke, baseball, and country music concerts.

Connect with June on LinkedIn at
https://www.linkedin.com/in/junejewell/

Made in United States
North Haven, CT
20 September 2023

41771732R00117